# PHILOSOPHY OF RELIGION

## A Universalist Perspective

## Marvin C. Sterling
University of the District of Columbia

UNIVERSITY
PRESS OF
AMERICA

Lanham • New York • London

**Library of Congress Cataloging-in-Publication Data**

Sterling, Marvin C.
Philosophy of religion : a universalist perspective /
Marvin C. Sterling.
p.    cm.
Includes bibliographical references and index.
1. Religion—Philosophy.   2. Religions (Proposed, universal, etc.)
I. Title.
BL51.S656      1992      200'.1—dc20      92–29528  CIP

ISBN 0–8191–8886–7 (cloth : alk. paper)
ISBN 0–8191–8887–5 (pbk. : alk. paper)

DEDICATED TO:

My wife, Effie Sterling
My son, Jimmy Sterling
My son, Chris Sterling
My daughter, Shellie Sterling

# ACKNOWLEDGMENTS

I would like to express my gratitude towards my parents (and more remote ancestors) for making it possible for me to be here to undertake this work.

My thanks to Ozzie Aghazadeh, my sister-in-law. If not for her generosity (specifically her gift of a word processor), I might have remained content with my obsolescent typewriter for completion of the entire book.

I wish to express my gratitude to Claire Wilson, of Claire Wilson and Associates in Washington, D.C., for typing a portion of the manuscript, and for answering a host of questions--which I had at various stages of the writing--concerning the use of computers.

I would also like to thank Dr. Terry L. Smith, former Chairperson of UDC's Department of Philosophy, for his perceptive comments on Chapter 8 (The Brain-Dependency Argument [against survival]). He offered a critique of that chapter from the standpoint of his own metaphysical materialism; and, as a result of reflecting on his remarks, I came to realize that, in order to give the fairest possible representation of the brain-dependency argument (prior to my attempt at refuting it) I would have to make a significant addition to that chapter.

I am also indebted to my colleague Claudette Jones, of UDC's Department of Philosophy. The invariably thought-provoking discussions which we have occasionally engaged in between classes have doubtless impacted on the writing of this book in a positive way.

A special thanks to Dr. David D. Barnett (of UDC's Department of Computer Science), from whose expertise I profited in the course of preparing corrected laser prints for UPA.

Finally, I would like to acknowledge the kind assistance of Joseph "Tex" Gathings, Associate Dean of UDC's College of Liberal and Fine Arts. He has been incredibly generous with his time in helping me to prepare the final, "camera-ready" copy of the manuscript for submission to UPA. Considering his busy schedule as dean, I am especially appreciative of his assistance.

# TABLE OF CONTENTS

CHAPTER ONE:


A UNIVERSALIST PERSPECTIVE
ON RELIGIONS

CHAPTER ONE:   A Universalist Perspective on Religions

What is the basic meaning of the word "God?"  If there really is a God, what is "he" like?  Is God a person, or simply some sort of impersonal force?  How can the existence of God be rationally proven?  What are the main arguments that are commonly appealed to by those who deny that God exists?  What happens when we die?  What is the essence or true being of persons?  Is the real person a soul, a body, or a combination of the two?  What exactly is a *spiritual* being?  If there really is life after death, how can this be rationally proven?  What are the principal arguments that are commonly invoked by those who try to show that there is no life after death?  Such questions concerning God, the soul, and life after death fall within the sphere of concern of the philosophy of religion.  Philosophy of religion seeks to clarify and evaluate the key concepts of religion, generally speaking, as well as those which are uniquely characteristic of particular religious traditions.

This introduction to the philosophy of religion is written from a *universalist* perspective.  By "*universalist perspective*" I mean the point of view of one who sees an underlying harmony between the different religions of the world, and who is disposed to emphasize their points of agreement.  This book bears the subtitle, *A Universalist Perspective*, because it reflects in a clear fashion my own philosophically-grounded conviction that each of the following propositions is worthy of being taken seriously:

(1)  The world that is revealed to us through the functioning of our five bodily senses is not the whole of Reality, but rather merely one portion of a much larger total Existence; in other words, there exists a *supersensible* world, a world which transcends, or is altogether distinct from, the visible one which appears to us in consequence of the reactions of our eyes (and other bodily senses).

(2)  This supersensible world is inhabited by intelligent beings.

(3)  Some of the inhabitants of the supersensible world are advanced in wisdom (i.e., in the knowledge of eternal spiritual truth) to an extent that greatly surpasses that which is normally attainable by inhabitants of the sense-perceptible world.

(4)  Important information regarding spiritual (and other) matters is sometimes transmitted from inhabitants of the supersensible world to inhabitants of the sense-perceptible world.

(5)  The central teachings of the major world religions consist of information of the sort mentioned in (4), that is, information which has been transmitted by inhabitants of the supersensible world to receptive individuals inhabiting the sense-perceptible world.

(6)  Because they have originated from the same source, and describe the same Reality, these religions all have in common the same basic teachings.

(7)  In addition to the central teachings which the various religious traditions all have in common, each religion also comprises more peripheral teachings which differentiate it from other religions.

(8)  The special teachings of each religion by which it is distinguished from others also consist of information that has been transmitted from inhabitants of the supersensible world to individuals inhabiting the sense-perceptible world.

(9)  Where the religions differ in their teachings, it is almost

invariably because such teachings either (a) give information about different facets of the same Reality, and are thus mutually compatible even though different, or (b) result from distortions of the original supersensible transmission due to limited and widely differing receptive capacities among inhabitants of the sense-perceptible world.

I have alluded to my conviction that the above nine propositions are worthy of being taken seriously. But, what rational justification is there for making such a claim? That is, what grounds are there for believing that these nine propositions are likely to be true? Establishing the truth of these nine propositions is not among the primary objectives of this introduction to the philosophy of religion; my main reason for listing them here is that the universalist perspective which they define is a determinant of the overall character of this work. Nevertheless, throughout this book, much of what is to be said in the way of argumentation will have a confirmatory relevance  to these nine propositions. For example, I shall attempt to argue in favor of a certain theory of sense-perception, and shall maintain that--in light of the truth of this theory--proposition (1) above is highly probable. Moreover, propositions (2) and (3) will be seen to be plausible as logical consequences of a certain metaphysical position which is strongly suggested by this theory of sense-perception. Finally, I submit that propositions (4) through (9) may be regarded as hypotheses in terms of which we can explain certain facts pertaining to the nature and inter-relations of the major world religions.

The universalist perspective set forth in the above nine propositions may be clarified further by the use of a comparison. In this connection, I wish to employ--in modified form--a well-known story recounted by the Sufi thinker Jalal-i-Din Rumi. In his book, the *Masnavi*, Rumi relates the following:

Some Hindoos were exhibiting an elephant in a dark room, and many people collected to see it. But as the place was too dark to permit them to see the elephant, they all felt it with their hands, to gain an idea of what it was like. One felt its trunk, and declared that the beast resembled a water-pipe; another felt its ear, and said it must be a large fan; another its leg, and thought it must be a pillar; another felt its back, and declared the beast must be like a great throne. According to the part which each felt, he gave a different description of the animal.[1]

Rumi wishes us to take the elephant in this story as representing higher spiritual Reality, and the persons in the dark room as standing for ordinary human beings limited to the common modes of knowing. Through this comparison he seeks to illustrate how it is possible for individuals whose powers of observation are restricted, and whose points of access differ, to say seemingly contradictory things about one and the same Reality.

I would like to modify and develop Rumi's comparison, in order further to elucidate the nine-point "universalist perspective" delineated above. Let us imagine that the elephant is located at the center of an enormous tent. This tent is circular in shape. Moreover, the tent is not a dark room; rather, its interior is fully illuminated. Also standing at the center, surrounding the elephant, are three individuals who are perfectly sighted, whose vision is in no way obstructed, and who are intimately familiar with the elephant's nature. These three individuals do not leave their positions near the elephant. A second group within the tent consists of a large number of individuals who are blindfolded. These blindfolded individuals have been tent-dwellers since birth, but have never seen any of the contents of the tent, due to the obstruction of their vision. They are able to move about freely in the tent; however, it just happens that the majority of them never approach the center where the elephant is located. Thus, individuals in this second group do not normally become acquainted with the nature of the elephant (not even in that minimal degree which would be possible through use of their sense of touch). Nevertheless, scattered throughout the tent are many tables, chairs, and other objects which these blindfolded individuals do become acquainted with, since they constantly encounter them as they move about in the tent. Let us assume that these objects are all--though in varying degrees--quite fragile as compared with the elephant. Moreover, all of these blindfolded individuals, on the basis of their tactual experience, sooner or later come to the realization that these objects which they commonly encounter in the tent are essentially perishable, and thus cannot be relied on indefinitely.

Now imagine that one of these blindfolded persons--in the course of moving about in the tent--happens to come near to one of the sighted persons positioned around the elephant. The sighted person immediately grabs hold of the blindfolded person   and emphatically states the following:  "There stands in your midst a great reality; this reality, unlike the objects with which you are currently familiar, is not fragile, but rather, a very stable and enduring reality; this reality is mighty and powerful; and it is a potential source of marvelous benefits for you, and for your fellow tent-dwellers; therefore, you must seek to familiarize yourself with this great reality, and also to inform your fellows of its existence and nature."   Having said the foregoing, the sighted person proceeds forcibly to tear away the blindfold from the eyes of this individual who has come near to him.

Being dazzled by the newly evident brightness of the tent's interior, the formerly blindfolded person is initially unable to see clearly what is in front of him.  But the two of them happen to be standing right next to the elephant's trunk, and the newly sighted tent-dweller--using both his sense of sight and touch--eventually succeeds in becoming acquainted in some degree with that part of the elephant which he experiences, namely the trunk.  His faculty of vision no longer obstructed, he now contemplates the bright spectacle of the tent's interior with great awe, and with a new enthusiasm for his existence.  However, like the emancipated cave-dweller of Plato's famous allegory, he feels pity for those individuals who still grope about in the tent blindfolded, and whose condition of deprivation is rendered all the more tragic by the fact that they are wholly unaware of the comparative poverty of their own experience.

Now, he does not have sufficient strength to tear away the blindfolds from the eyes of his fellow tent-dwellers.  Nonetheless, he does heed the counsel of his deliverer, and thus firmly resolves to devote himself to teaching those who are still blindfolded.  He teaches them concerning the elephant, stressing particularly its abiding quality, i.e., its superior endurance.  In fact, in this teaching activity he uses the same sequence of statements made earlier by the sighted person who removed his blindfold.  Moreover, in attempting to communicate his own experience of the elephant, he tries to connect it with something with which the tent--dwellers are already familiar through their tactual experience.  More specifically, since the particular part of the elephant of which he has gained some knowledge is the trunk, he says that the "great reality" concerning which he speaks is something like a "waterpipe."   Those tent-dwellers who accept his teachings, having organized themselves into a distinct community, come to be known as "Waterpipists." And the collective body of his teachings comes to be referred to as "Water-pipism." However, despite the efforts of the Waterpipists to spread their message, many of the tent-dwellers are not reached, and some of those who are reached are not willing to accept this message. Consequently, a considerable number of tent-dwellers remain outside of the organized community of Waterpipists.

Now, let us suppose that a second individual from among the blindfolded tent-dwellers happens to come near to one of the sighted persons who stand around the elephant. As in the previous case, the sighted person seizes this individual; makes the same sequence of statements regarding the greatness and durability of the elephant; and finally tears away his blindfold. In this case, however, let us imagine that the two of them happen to be standing near one of the elephant's hindlegs. Again, though dazzled by the sudden illumination, the newly seeing person succeeds in familiarizing himself with that part of the elephant which he experiences. As in the former case, this individual feels moved to return to his fellow tent-dwellers who are still blindfolded. He undertakes to educate them concerning the "new" reality to which he has gained access. All things unfold pretty much the way they did in the earlier case, with one noteworthy exception. This latest teacher declares that the reality concerning which he speaks is something like a great pillar; for in trying to communicate to his fellows his own experience of the elephant, he--like the previous teacher--desires to compare it to something with which they already have some acquaintance through touching. Accordingly, the followers of the new teacher, having established themselves as an organized community, come to be known as "Pillarists." His teachings, moreover, are collectively referred to as "Pillarism."

Finally, let us assume that a third individual from among these groping tent-dwellers chances to come near to one of the sighted persons surrounding the elephant. Imagine, moreover, that everything proceeds in the same manner as in the previous two cases, except for the fact that this individual glimpses a part of the elephant different from those formerly glimpsed. Let us suppose that, in this case, the part of the elephant of which some knowledge is gained is the elephant's back. Accordingly, this third teacher seeks to convey some idea of what he has experienced by comparing it to a "great throne." In consequence of his teaching activity, a community is established whose members are called "Thronists," and his teachings are collectively referred to as "Thronism."

Let us stipulate one further development in connection with the three "isms" mentioned above. Specifically, let us assume that differing conceptions of the elephant arise *within* each of the three communities. We may take these differences of conception to result from the fact that the blindfolded tent-dwellers have no direct experience of the elephant and are disposed to use tactual imagination (i.e., the mental imagery they form based on their touch-sensations) in order to eke out the basic idea of the elephant which was conveyed to them by their respective teachers. Let us suppose, moreover, that these differences of opinion become so extreme, in some instances, that they lead to the division of the major "isms" into sects (or "denominations").

According to the universalist perspective--on which the character and content of this book largely depend--the major world religions may be viewed as relating to one another in very much the same way that the three aforementioned "isms" relate to one another. Just as the "isms" of the tent-dwellers arose from the same source, and were attempts at describing the same reality, so also--according to the universalist perspective under consideration--such religions as Hinduism, Buddhism, Confucianism, Taoism, Christianity, and Islam have originated from a common source, and seek to communicate important truths concerning one and the same Reality.

Let us briefly note the main symbolic import of the various elements set forth in the imaginary situation we have depicted. The contents of the tent represent the whole of existence. The elephant stands for God, that is, the Universal Reality or Ultimate Truth of things. The three sighted persons surrounding the elephant represent the multitude of "angelic" beings (i.e., highly developed, spiritual beings) who populate the supersensible regions of existence. The many blindfolded persons stand for the ordinary human beings in this sense-perceptible world who remain restricted to the common modes of knowing. The tables, chairs, and other fragile objects in the tent represent the ever-changing, composite things which are revealed to us through ordinary sense-experience. The sense of touch of the tent-dwellers represents the five bodily senses (sight, hearing, etc.) generally operative among human beings as sources of knowledge about the world. The tent-dwellers' sense of sight stands for a putative higher faculty within us, through which we have the possibility of coming to know God intimately, and of understanding abstruse matters regarding the soul and its immortality. The state of being blindfolded stands for the condition prevailing among the masses of human beings in which the putative higher faculty remains dormant, that is, inactive. The state of being unblindfolded represents the condition of individuals in whom the "slumbering" higher faculty has been awakened or rendered "operational." The three teachers who established the Waterpipist, Pillarist, and Thronist communities represent such religion-founders as Krishna, Buddha, Christ, and Muhammad.

There is one additional point that should be made with a view to clarifying the universalist perspective underlying this book. That point is the following: In one important sense of the word "religion," there obviously CANNOT BE many religions, but rather ONE religion only, and all of the elements that constitute this one religion must be in mutual agreement. For, if higher spiritual Reality does exist, then, if we take "religion" in its most encompassing sense as meaning the total body of true information concerning this Reality, it follows that for there to be *many* religions is an impossibility, since there cannot be more than one set of propositions conforming to the description "total body of true information concerning higher spiritual Reality." In other words, the fact of totality would preclude the possibility of many-ness. There could not be *many* religions, each one of which was the TOTAL body of true information concerning higher spiritual Reality.

Furthermore, every conceivable belief-system consisting of a sub-set of the teachings of this one religion would necessarily be consistent with all other conceivable belief-systems which consisted of sub-sets of the teachings of this one religion. Such belief-systems could not contain conflicting claims; they could not be mutually contradictory. For, if higher spiritual Reality does exist, then all of the facts pertaining to it must of necessity be mutually compatible; this is patently true, since all such facts would actually be in *existence together*. In other words, if God, the soul, heaven, hell, etc. really do exist, then the total set of facts pertaining to them has an objective status in its own right, and its various elements constitute a coherent whole. Now, let us move from the objective facts to the cognitive representation of these facts, that is, to the inner conceptions of knowing individuals. Religious knowledge is an interior portrayal of religious facts; it is a depiction of such facts through

the human power of cognition. Religion, in the sense under consideration, is an all-inclusive portrayal of the objective facts pertaining to
higher spiritual Reality. Moreover, there is a parallelism or correspondence between objective facts and the interior representation of such
facts. Consequently, just as all of the objective facts that pertain to Spirit
are mutually *compatible*, so also the individual propositions (i.e., "pieces"
of true information) which depict these facts must all be mutually
*consistent*. Accordingly, the teachings of the "one religion" must
constitute a coherent set of propositions, and each conceivable sub-set of
its teachings must of necessity be in agreement with all other conceivable
sub-sets of its teachings.

An important implication of the universalist perspective which we are
trying to clarify is that each of the major world religions--conceived as a
distinctive combination of teachings--relates to the "one religion" as part
relates to whole. In other words, though there are varying degrees of
overlap between the teachings that constitute Hinduism, Buddhism,
Judaism, Christianity, and Islam, nonetheless, each one of these
belief-systems may be viewed as a certain unique sub-set of the total set
of propositions that constitute the "one religion." More precisely, the
universalist perspective maintains that if each of the several religions
could be wholly purified of the fringe of inaccuracies that has arisen
within it, due to the circumscribed scope of the experience of its
followers (i.e., due to the limited "reach" of their perception), then each
religion could be seen as being the presentation of a certain portion of the
TOTAL TRUTH. Moreover, if this were actually the case, then--in view
of the points made earlier--these purified forms of the major world
religions would have to be in complete agreement with one another.

If we conceive of the various religions along the lines indicated
above, i.e., as parts of one whole, then what must we conclude with
regard to the *mutual condemnation* and *excessive proselytizing* which
sometimes characterize their inter-relations? Let us think of the matter in
metaphorical terms.

When we find instances in which Christians, Muslims, Buddhists, or
other religious persons, are disposed to hate and reject one another, this is
about as reasonable as it would be for the brain, heart, lungs, and other
parts of the body to be involved in mutual hostility and conflict.
Furthermore, overly vigorous attempts at converting others to one's own

religion are--on this view--just as inappropriate as it would be if the brain were to insist that the heart, lungs, and other organs should all be transformed into brains, or if any other bodily organs were to make a similar demand. If the whole human body were transformed into a lung, would that be in any sense a desirable result? Would it be at all felicitous, if the body in its entirety were to become a liver, or one large muscle? This analogy is perhaps somewhat crude; nonetheless, it provides an effective means by which important implications of a universalist perspective on religions can be more fully appreciated.

This last series of points which I have attempted to make in connection with the universalist perspective from which this book has been written is very neatly summed up in a certain saying of the Theosophists: "There is no religion higher than Truth."

In conclusion, it is worth noting that the above-characterized universalist perspective is by no means new. On the contrary, there have always been at least a few individuals within every major religion who have--with varying degrees of explicitness--endorsed such a perspective. However, among those forces currently working for the dissemination of universalist insights on religion, the Baha'i movement, dating from roughly the middle of the 19th century, is perhaps the most salient.

*Notes*

[1]*The Masnavi*: Translated & Abridged by E.H. Whinfield (New York: E.P. Dutton & Co., Inc., 1975), p. 12.

CHAPTER TWO:

WHAT IS PHILOSOPHY OF RELIGION?

CHAPTER TWO: What is Philosophy of Religion?

In this chapter we shall address the question, "What is philosophy of religion?" To begin with, however, we may focus on the more basic question, "What is philosophy?" For philosophy of religion is a branch of philosophy, and consequently, to do philosophy of religion is simply to do a particular *kind* of philosophy.

During the latter part of the 19th century, and throughout the early decades of the 20th century, the question, "What is philosophy?" became increasingly a matter of controversy among large numbers of Western philosophers. Philosophers disagreed vehemently among themselves as to what the true nature and task of philosophy was. However, if we look at this period of disagreement within the context of the entire history of philosophy--which stretches back to several hundred years before the birth of Christ--we are compelled to admit that it was a very brief period indeed. For the most part, philosophers have been, and continue to be, basically in agreement as regards the nature and task of philosophy. Accordingly, the account of philosophy presented in what follows will be developed along traditional lines; it could be described as a *conservative* view of philosophy.

## What is Philosophy?

Perhaps the best way of setting about to clarify this traditional view of philosophy is to call attention to the etymology of the word. The word "philosophy" is derived from the Greek words "philos" and "sophia." These words mean, respectively, *loving* and *wisdom*. Thus, in keeping with the etymology of the word, it could be said that philosophy is simply love of wisdom, and a philosopher is one who loves wisdom.

Now, loving something is inseparably bound up with SEEKING that something. To say that we love a thing necessarily implies that we are disposed to seek it out. Moreover, the connection between loving and seeking is the key thing to note in our attempt at clarifying what philosophy is. In fact, the etymological account of philosophy may alternatively be formulated as follows: Philosophy is the systematic pursuit of wisdom, i.e., it consists in a deliberate and orderly seeking out of wisdom.

Viewed in this light, philosophy is seen to be a certain kind of ACTIVITY, viz., the activity of seeking wisdom. However, if we consider the full range of differing contexts in which the word "philosophy" is used, we discover that it is ambiguous. The word sometimes refers to the mentioned activity, but it equally frequently designates the goal of this activity. To be more explicit, the word "philosophy" sometimes refers to the activity of SEEKING wisdom; it sometimes designates the WISDOM sought; and on other occasions, BOTH meanings are intended simultaneously. Now, within the context of the expression "philosophy of religion," the word "philosophy" refers primarily to the activity of SEEKING. Consequently, it is on this sense of the word that we will focus in the ensuing discussion.

With regard to the matter of seeking, another point needs to be emphasized. It is not just any instance of seeking wisdom that can rightly be characterized as philosophy. For, insofar as several different ways of attaining wisdom are conceivable, only those ways which rely primarily on THINKING may legitimately be regarded as amounting to philosophy. That is, philosophy is the pursuit of wisdom *by means of thinking*; or, alternatively expressed, it is in itself deliberate and orderly THINKING which is engaged in for the purpose of attaining wisdom.

Thus, an assumption which underlies the philosophic enterprise is that a certain type of knowledge, at least, can be gained purely by means of thinking. But what justification is there for this assumption? A detailed answer to this question is beyond the scope of this book. Nonetheless, it would be useful here to address the matter briefly. In attempting to do this, the chief point that needs to be stressed is that in the inner world of ideas there is, so to speak, a certain interconnectedness. That is, single ideas do not stand in absolute isolation from one another, rather they naturally "cohere," or "lead into" one another, in a manner comparable to that in which the different links in a chain may be said to "cohere" or to "lead into" one another. In philosophy, thinking proceeds in an orderly way from one idea to another, and from single ideas to progressively more inclusive ideational complexes. Moreover, it is through taking note of the natural connections between ideas that thinking is able to accomplish this. Now assume that in addition to these interconnections WITHIN the world of ideas, there is also a kind of conformity of this inner world of ideas with the outer world of facts. It is then by virtue of this conformity that we are able, purely by means of thinking, to arrive at genuine insights about the external universe of facts. As is frequently noted, something similar happens in geometry when, for example, we think out the implications of the idea of a triangle, i.e., when through thinking alone we discover progressively more and more of what must be the case with respect to all triangles.

Let us try to be a bit more explicit. There are certain essential inter-connections among the various facts of the external world, and the structure and interconnectedness of these outer facts CORRESPOND to the structure and interconnectedness that characterize the inner ideas. Moreover, by thinking alone we can discover the essential ties that exist between different ideas. Now it is obvious that such discoveries amount to gaining knowledge about the inner world of ideas. However, the important thing to note is that the knowledge gained in this way is not only knowledge about the inner world of ideas; rather, it constitutes at the same time knowledge concerning the external universe of facts. For--we may suppose--there is a correspondence, an isomorphism, between the two. Let us employ a somewhat crude, though potentially illuminating, comparison. Keeping in mind that the following is only an analogy, imagine yourself to be standing facing a large mirror with a great many objects positioned behind you. If you look into the mirror in order to determine the character and interrelationships of the images that you see there, you will gain knowledge not only about the mirror-images as such, but also of the objects positioned behind you.

Two main points should be extracted from the foregoing: (1) Philosophy may be defined as deliberate and orderly THINKING which is engaged in for the attainment of WISDOM; and (2) The attainment of objective knowledge purely by means of thinking is a real possibility.

So far, in attempting to unpack some of the implications of the etymological account of philosophy, we have been concerned exclusively with its reference to love. That is, we first noted that, etymologically speaking, philosophy is love of wisdom, and then we proceeded to consider the significance of the word "love" in this context. But now, granting that philosophy is thinking for the attainment of wisdom, we may still ask: "What is wisdom?" This is the question we need briefly to consider next.

In addressing this question, let us begin with what is most obvious, specifically, with the observation that wisdom is knowledge. For this much at least seems uncontroversial. Moreover, just as it is clear that wisdom is knowledge, it is also clear that wisdom is not just any knowledge; rather, it is a certain sort of knowledge. In other words, every instance of what is correctly referred to as wisdom is necessarily an instance of knowledge, but not every instance of what is rightly designated as knowledge is necessarily an instance of wisdom.

Now, given that wisdom is a particular kind of knowledge, we may ask the further question "What is it that differentiates those cases of knowledge which qualify as wisdom from those cases of knowledge which do not qualify as wisdom?" What is it, in other words, that sets wisdom apart as a special case of knowledge? One of the numerous ways in which we could word the reply to this is as follows: Wisdom is not just any knowledge, rather it is specifically knowledge concerning *Ultimate Reality* and *Ultimate Goodness*. We may understand the adjective "ultimate" here to signify "essential and, hence, inalterable." Thus, possessing wisdom involves having discernment with respect to essential-inalterable BEING and essential-inalterable VALUE. Accordingly, wisdom may be said to include the knowledge of how to distinguish between the real and the unreal. It is to know--among other things--the true nature of the "self," of one's own "I." To be wise is to be acquainted with the *fundamental* character of the world, and with the status of the "I" in relation to the world. It is--among other things--to be informed as to that which is good in the highest degree, and includes the ability to distinguish between the greater good and the lesser good. Wisdom consists in knowing how to choose and how to live. To be wise is to know the meaning of existence, and thus, the supreme goal of human life.

## Three Senses of "Wisdom"

Let us consider just a few additional points regarding wisdom. We have seen that wisdom is a particular kind of knowledge. But "knowledge" may be understood in at least three different senses. Specifically, we may distinguish between the *ideational* sense, the *episodic* sense, and the *dispositional* sense of the word "knowledge." These three senses of "knowledge" need to be clarified in turn. For, the word "wisdom" has a similar pattern of ambiguity, that is, it is characterized by the same threefold employment.

In the ideational sense of the word, knowledge consists of propositions. A proposition is a single "piece" of information; or, more precisely, it is the underlying idea which is expressed by a declarative sentence. One way in which the term "proposition" is sometimes elucidated is by pointing to a set of sentences such as the one below. The following are four DIFFERENT sentences, but these different sentences all convey the SAME proposition:

(1)  The door is open.
(2)  La puerta esta abierta. (SPANISH)
(3)  La porte est ouverte. (FRENCH)
(4)  Die Tür ist aufgemacht. (GERMAN)

All of the above sentences express one and the same idea, and this idea is an example of what is meant by "proposition."

In the episodic sense of the word, knowledge consists of actual mental performances, certain acts of the mind. (The adjective "episodic" signifies in this context: pertaining to an episode or actual occurrence.) In this sense, the act-of-entertaining a given proposition could count as knowledge. To entertain a proposition is to hold that proposition in mind; it is to THINK that proposition or to REALIZE it. It is surely necessary to make a distinction between any given proposition that is entertained on the one hand, and the act of entertaining that proposition on the other. Moreover, this distinction can be acknowledged without one's needing to take any position whatever as to the specific nature of the relationship between the two. One could remain wholly non-committal on the question as to how exactly the act of entertaining a proposition relates to the proposition entertained. However, it is plausible to maintain that the relationship between the two is that of the internal accusative of an action to the action of which it is the internal accusative. Let us try to arrive at greater clarity in this matter.

The grammatical term "accusative," strictly speaking, is an appellation for any *word* which functions as the direct object of a given verb. Nevertheless, by extension, I use the term "accusative" more loosely here to mention also the *referents* of such direct object words. Take the sentence "He reads the Bible daily." On this loose employment of the term "accusative," we can say not only that the *word* "Bible" is the accusative of the verb "reads," but also that the *thing* that "Bible" refers to (i.e., the actual book) is the accusative of the *action* of reading.

Now accusatives can be divided into two groups, namely *external* accusatives and *internal* accusatives. Consider the statement "He played the violin." Here, the action is playing, and its accusative is that which is played, i.e., the violin. Moreover, since the violin stands in relation to the playing as a thing wholly separate and distinct, we can say that the violin is the external accusative of the playing. But consider the statement "He ran the race." In this case, the action is running, and its accusative is that which is run, namely, the race. However, the race is not something separate and distinct from the running; rather, the race is indefeasibly tied to the act of running. And because the race is, so to speak, "internal" to the action, it exemplifies what is meant by an internal accusative. Similarly, in the statements "He did ten push-ups," and "They danced the waltz," the push-ups and the waltz are internal accusatives of the respective actions.

To return to the main point, it could be maintained that *propositions* entertained stand in relation to the corresponding acts-of-entertaining as internal accusatives to the actions of which they are the internal accusatives. Nonetheless, it should be stressed that it is not necessary that one adopt this particular view of the relationship in order to recognize the basic distinction. For to see that a proposition entertained is one thing, and the act of entertaining it another, is considerably easier than seeing precisely what sort of relationship exists between the two.

Let us now consider the third sense of "knowledge" alluded to above, i.e., the dispositional. In its dispositional sense, the word "knowledge" applies to a particular kind of power. In order to get clear concerning knowledge in this sense of the word, let us consider the pertinent points regarding power. Every mental ACT is the expression of underlying mental POWER. Moreover, no act could ever actually OCCUR if the corresponding power did not PRE-EXIST. That is, if the corresponding power did not already exist PRIOR TO the occurrence of a given act, then that act could never occur. For, to PERFORM an act just is to EXERCISE the corresponding power, i.e., to manifest or show forth such power. Furthermore, power is definitely something different from all conceivable acts which express it. As support for this, consider, for instance, that mental power--in itself--can never actually be observed, whereas mental acts are introspectively observable. (For example, I cannot observe my *ability* to form visual images, since the ability itself is purely intelligible; however, I can observe the actual *visual images* which express, or reveal, this ability.) Thus, the very occurrence of a mental act forces us to posit POWER that is distinct from that act. In other words, we cannot explain the occurrence of a mental act without appealing to the notion of pre-existing POWER; rather, based on the very occurrence of a mental act, we must assume that the corresponding power was already A FACT (was already IN EXISTENCE) before that mental act occurred. For, a mental act is simply the episodic manifestation of a certain kind of power, a showing forth of power in an actual occurrence.

Now, any given act-of-entertaining-a-proposition, which constitutes knowledge in the episodic sense of the word, is an instance of showing-forth-power-in-an-actual-occurrence. And this underlying power--which is equally present whether or not it is actually manifested--is what is meant by knowledge in the dispositional sense of the word. If, in the dispositional sense, we know that Washington is the capital of the United States, then it is correct for one to say that we possess this knowledge, whether or not we happen to be entertaining the relevant proposition, that is, whether or not we happen to be actually holding in mind the idea that Washington is the capital of the United States. In other words, in the dispositional sense, we know that Washington is the capital of the United States, even when we happen not to be thinking about this fact; for the knowledge is still present in the form of power.

To recapitulate, the word "knowledge" has a threefold employment. Sometimes it refers to *information known*; at other times it designates actual *acts of knowing* such information; and on still other occasions it means the *power to perform* such acts of knowing. Information known constitutes knowledge in the ideational sense. Actual acts of knowing such information constitute knowledge in the episodic sense. And the power to perform such acts of knowing constitutes knowledge in the dispositional sense.

We noted earlier that wisdom is definable as knowledge concerning Ultimate Reality and Ultimate Goodness. Moreover, the same threefold employment which is applicable in connection with knowledge, generally speaking, also applies to wisdom as a special case of knowledge. Accordingly, we may distinguish between an ideational sense, an episodic sense, and a dispositional sense of the word "wisdom."

We saw at the outset that philosophy can be defined as THINKING for the attainment of WISDOM. A more explicit definition is now possible in the light of the foregoing. Philosophy consists in deliberate and orderly THINKING that is engaged in for the purpose of attaining KNOWLEDGE concerning Ultimate Reality and Ultimate Goodness. This knowledge of the ultimately real and good--which constitutes what is called WISDOM--is the goal of philosophy in all three senses clarified above. Let us briefly elaborate on this latter point.

Philosophic thinking--beginning with definitely articulated problems--first of all arrives at specific propositions which purport to be solutions to these problems. Such propositions, if correct, constitute wisdom in the ideational sense of the word. Moreover, the very fact of arriving at such propositions is inseparably bound up with entertaining them or holding them in mind. These acts of entertaining propositions constitute wisdom in the episodic sense of the word. Lastly, an initial act of entertaining such propositions tends toward an awakening--so to speak--of the underlying power of which the act is an expression. Furthermore, each subsequent act of entertaining such propositions (i.e., each repeated act of cognizing) has the effect of further awakening this underlying power, thereby facilitating and strengthening the performance of future acts of cognition. This underlying power--especially insofar as it has actually been "awakened"--is what is meant by wisdom in the dispositional sense of the word. The upshot of these remarks is that the reference to wisdom in the definition of philosophy encompasses all three senses previously discussed.

## Philosophy of Religion

The question raised at the very beginning of this chapter may now be answered as follows. In the expression "philosophy of religion" the word "philosophy" signifies deliberate and orderly THINKING, engaged in for the attainment of WISDOM, that is, in order to arrive at knowledge about Ultimate Reality and Ultimate Goodness. When we add "of religion" to this, the entire resulting expression still refers to such THINKING, but only insofar as it (i.e., the THINKING) seeks to achieve its aim by focusing specifically on RELIGIOUS TEACHINGS. This assumes of course that knowledge of religious teachings counts as wisdom. To be more explicit, philosophy *of religion* is distinguished from other varieties of philosophizing by having as its immediate goals CLARIFICATION of the deeper meaning of religious teachings, and DETERMINATION of their truth or plausibility. Thus, in doing philosophy of religion, an attempt is made to unpack the full implications of notions such as God, Brahman, Allah, creation, providence, karma, soul, spirit, atman, resurrection, reincarnation, heaven, etc.; moreover, an attempt is made to discover to what extent acceptance of such ideas is rationally justified.

CHAPTER THREE:


THE CONCEPT OF GOD

CHAPTER THREE: The Concept of God

There are many different ways of thinking about God. If we could look into the minds of any randomly selected set of believers, we would very likely find that they harbored strikingly different ideas about God. Such differences would probably be noted even in cases where the individuals selected all belonged to the same religion. But in spite of the great diversity which obtains among the views held by different individuals on the matter of what God is like, it seems clear that there is a common thread which unites these differing views. In other words, there is a central component, a foundation-idea, so to speak, which is shared in common by these divergent ways of thinking about God.

God, the Supreme Being

In this chapter, we will attempt to get clear concerning this innermost core of the concept of God. Subsequently, we will examine some of the major alternative ways of conceiving of God. And finally, an effort will be made to assess the plausibility of these differing views of what God is like. Moreover, in seeking to accomplish this latter objective, we shall have occasion to look more deeply into the basic idea of God, and to unfold more of its implicit content. For, in this way, it will be possible to adduce rational support for the conclusions to be advanced as to the merits of these differing views of God.

In reviewing the history of thought, we encounter numerous formulas that have been proposed as ways of capturing the basic meaning of the word "God." To mention just a few examples, it has been stated that

God is "the all-perfect-being," "the absolutely necessary being," "the sufficient reason of things," "that than which nothing greater can be conceived," and so forth. I wish to suggest that most of these historically encountered definitions are basically sound. For, even though they differ among themselves, nonetheless each of these traditional definitions of God tends to highlight some limited idea which is, in fact, a portion or aspect of the overall concept. In particular, if we begin with any one of these traditional definitions, we will ordinarily be able--through sustained analysis--to arrive at the content of the others; and, speaking more generally, by following out the implications of the aspect highlighted by a given definition, further aspects of the overall concept can be uncovered. Thus, it really does not matter very much which particular formulation we begin with.

Let us employ as our point of departure one of the most widely recognized characterizations of God, viz., "supreme being." One frequently hears it said that God is the supreme being. And to say this is actually to take hold of the very heart of the concept of God. Let us seek additional light on this matter through ferreting out the logical consequences of the basic concept. The two components of the locution may be considered in turn.

### An Explication of "Supreme Being"

Let us start with "being." What is the significance of the word "being" within the context of the statement "God is the supreme being"? There is no need for a lengthy reply to this, since the answer is pretty much clear without discussion. However, there is one point that may profitably be touched on. The word "being" is ambiguous; it is ordinarily used in one or the other of two main senses. "Being" is often understood to mean roughly "a living thing that is either person-like, or  that is actually a person." For example, consider the associations immediately evoked by the word "beings" when we hear the statement "You should not expect to find any beings on the planet Mars." We would normally take this as amounting to a denial that any living things are to be found on Mars, and we would specifically be led to think of the absence of all PERSONS (or person-like entities) from the surface of this planet. Let us call this the narrow sense of the word "being."

This narrow sense of the word is probably the one which is most frequently intended in common parlance. However, the word "being," as employed in the locution "supreme being," ought not to be understood in the narrow sense. For, ideally, an account of the basic meaning of the word "God" ought to be able--at least *prima facie*--to accommodate all of the major alternative views as to what God is like. (That is, even though a deep-probing analysis of such an account might lead us to choose some particular conception of God, and to reject all others, nevertheless, an accurate account of the basic meaning of the word "God" should not reduce any of the differing conceptions of God to an OBVIOUS absurdity. Now if we take "being" in the narrow sense of the word, then the resulting account of God as supreme being would not be able to accommodate all of the major divergent views of God, but rather would reduce some of these views to obvious absurdity. Therefore, as stated previously, the word "being" as used in the expression "supreme being" ought not to be understood in what we have termed the narrow sense of the word. Let us try to bring out the main points a bit more explicitly.

If any of the major alternative views as to what God is like were just OBVIOUSLY misguided, then it would not be possible for it to gain large numbers of supporters. However, all of the major divergent views as to what God is like have large numbers of supporters. Consequently, none of these differing views of God is just OBVIOUSLY misguided. Now, among the main divergent views of what God is like there are some which maintain that God is not a person, but rather a Reality of an altogether different sort. Thus, it would follow from the foregoing that those views which maintain that God is not a person are not just OBVIOUSLY misguided. That is, such impersonalist conceptions of God might ultimately turn out to be wrong, but--if so--their incorrectness cannot be something evident *prima facie*. But consider the following.

If we take "being" in the narrow sense of the word, then it is true by definition that the supreme being must be thought of as a person or as somehow person-like. Moreover, it would obviously follow that God--defined as "supreme being"--must be a person or somehow person-like. In other words, a logical consequence of taking "being" in the narrow sense would be to make the statement "God is a personal Reality" true by definition. And, assuming the narrow sense of "being," the statement "God is not a person" would be transparently contradictory. Accordingly, it would follow that any view maintaining that God is not a person is just OBVIOUSLY misguided. But, as emphasized above, none of the main divergent conceptions of what God is like-including impersonalist views--is just OBVIOUSLY misguided. Consequently, as employed in the expression "supreme being," the word "being" ought not to be taken in the narrow sense, but rather in a sense sufficiently broad to accommodate the varying views of God. In particular, "being" needs to be defined in such a way as to be neutral on the question of whether God is a personal or non-personal Reality. In this way, use of the term will not automatically amount to pre-judging the matter.

How, then, should we understand the word "being" within the context of the expression "supreme being?" To facilitate a clear statement of the answer to this, let us recall that the noun "being" is simply a particular form of the verb "to be." Consequently, the basic points that can be made regarding the verb "to be" have applicability, by extension, to the word "being" and to the numerous other forms of this verb. Now, if we conjugate the verb "to be" in the present tense, we obtain the forms "I am," "you are," "he is," and so on. Let us take the form "is" to make the general point I wish to set forth.

It is commonly noted by logicians and grammarians that the verb "to be" has three main senses; namely, a *predicative* sense, an *existential* sense, and an *identic* sense. Moreover, the form "is" reflects this basic fact of three senses. Employed in the predicative sense the verb "is" ascribes some quality or characteristic to a thing, whereas in its existential and identic senses--as the very names clearly indicate--it affirms existence and identity, respectively. Consider, for example, the following passage from the Bible: "But without faith *it is impossible* to please him: for he that cometh to God must believe that *he is*, and that *he is a rewarder* of them that diligently seek him." (Hebrews, 11:6; emphasis added.)

In the above verse from the Bible, the word "is" occurs in three places, specifically in the statements "It is impossible," "He is," and "He is a rewarder." In the statement "It is impossible," the verb "is" is used in its predicative sense, for here it ascribes impossibility to something (viz., to it, where "it" stands for pleasing God). In the statement "He is" we find the existential employment of "is," for in this statement it affirms existence. And the statement "He is a rewarder" illustrates the identic sense of "is," since in this case identity is being affirmed.

All three of these senses of the verb "to be" are applicable to the noun form "being." Moreover, the particular sense which is most pertinent to the expression "supreme being" is the EXISTENTIAL sense. But my purpose in calling attention to this is not primarily to exclude the other two senses, but rather to underscore the neutrality of the specific sense which is relevant. The main point to note here is that--within the context of the expression "supreme being"--the word "being" simply means that which IS, in the existential sense of "is." It is synonymous with such words as "Reality," "Entity," and--broadly construed--"Thing." It does not specifically signify a Reality, Entity, or Thing of some particular kind. When we say "being" in this existential sense of the word, the exact nature of what is referred to is left entirely open. It is especially important to note that such a referent could be either personal or non-personal in nature. If we understand the word "existent," not as an adjective, but rather as a noun, then we can say that the word "being," as used in the locution "supreme being," simply means Existent. This is the second, broader sense of the word "being," which was alluded to previously.

The other component of the locution "supreme being" is the adjective "supreme." When we define God as supreme being, what is the significance of the word "supreme?" The literal meaning of this word is simply *highest*. But clearly this literal meaning of "supreme" is not what is intended in the designation "supreme being." That is, to say that God is the supreme being obviously does not amount to saying that God is--strictly speaking--the highest Reality; for this would entail the fatuous view that God is that Something or Someone that occupies the furthest point reachable by traveling in an upward direction. And such a notion of God would be internally inconsistent, since the whole idea of a "furthest point reachable" is inseparably tied to the idea of space, and the very idea of space logically excludes the possibility of its having a furthest point reachable. Thus, obviously, to say that God is the supreme being is to speak metaphorically. It is to say that God is, not literally but rather figuratively speaking, the highest Reality. But what exactly is this figurative sense of the world "highest?"

If we reflect on the various contexts in which we speak figuratively of highness and lowness, it will become evident that the chief metaphorical function of these terms is to convey the idea of differences in rank. Rank, in turn, can normally be delimited by reference to two things, namely, extent of CONTROL exercised, and degree of VALUE or EXCELLENCE possessed. For instance, if we were to say that the president of a university is higher than its deans but occupies a lower position than its board of trustees, use of the words "higher" and "lower" would primarily call attention to the differing degrees of control exercised by those referred to. But when certain 19th century scholars spoke of higher and lower races, they wanted mainly to convey the false idea that differing degrees of value (or excellence) characterize the various racial groups into which humanity is divided. Moreover--in the figurative employment of "high" and "low"--both extent of control and degree of value are sometimes simultaneously intended.

Accordingly, the word "supreme," as employed in the expression "supreme being," signifies highest, that is, high in the greatest conceivable degree. And this maximal highness involves two things: (1) Exercising CONTROL to the greatest conceivable extent, and (2) Possessing EXCELLENCE to the greatest conceivable extent. Therefore, when we describe God as "supreme," this may be understood to mean that God is CAUSATIVE most *extensively*, and at the same time CAUSATIVE most *excellently*.

For, to say that God is causative most extensively is to say that God's control extends to ALL things, conditions, and occurrences; on the other hand, to say that God is causative most excellently (which follows inescapably from God's maximal excellence-possession) implies that God's control results exclusively in the BEST CONCEIVABLE things, conditions, and occurrences. To express this more concisely, if we stipulate for the adjective "superlative" the twofold meaning *extending to All and, at the same time, carried out in the BEST conceivable manner*, then we may simply say that God is superlatively causative. In other words, we can now define "supreme" as meaning *superlatively causative, that is, causative most extensively and at the same time most excellently.*

In accordance with the above, to say that God is the supreme being amounts to saying that God is the superlatively causative reality, i.e., that Something or Someone that causes all things, conditions, and occurrences, and moreover, causes only the best conceivable things, conditions, and occurrences. Let us make some further points concerning the two facets of superlative causation which we have noted. First, to be causative most extensively entails the following clearly distinguishable components: (1) Determination of the existence of all THINGS, and (2) Determination of the successive CONDITIONS and OCCURRENCES which things go through. Let us designate (1) as "creating," and (2) as "ruling." In keeping with this, we may say that two elements essential to the concept of God are CREATION and RULERSHIP. To say that God, the supreme being, exists is to say--among other things--that there exists a Something or Someone that is both creator of all things, and ruler over all things.

Now there may be differences of opinion as to the full significance of the idea that God creates things, and divergent views are also possible as to how, or whether, God's ruling over things can be reconciled with human free will. Nonetheless, the notions of creativity and rulership, *per se*, cannot logically be severed from the idea of God.

The other notion which we are considering is the idea of being causative most excellently. To be causative most excellently is to be the cause of the best conceivable things, conditions, and occurrences. Let us use the words "beauty" and "wealth" in connection with the things resulting from God's creating, and the word "desirability" with regard to the conditions and occurrences resulting from God's ruling. (The terms "beauty," "wealth," and "desirability" should be taken here in a very broad sense, and not merely sensually.) Now, to be beautiful is to have qualities the contemplation or consideration of which is a source of delight; whereas, to be wealthy is to own, that is, to have rightful access to the enjoyment of, an abundance of accumulated goods. Thus, maximal beauty consists in having all conceivable qualities the contemplation of which is a source of delight, and maximal wealth (i.e., "wealthiness") consists in owning, or having rightful access to, an all-encompassing abundance of goods. Now, using this terminology, we may say that, since the divine supremacy implies that God must be thought of as most excellently causative, it follows that God causes only those things which are maximally beautiful and maximally wealthy. Similarly, it follows that God causes only those conditions and occurrences which are maximally desirable. That is, the events and circumstances arising through God's rulership must all have a character such as would evoke the approval of a fully rational being who contemplated them.

Let us recapitulate. "God" may be defined as the supreme being. It follows from this that if something actually exists corresponding to this concept, then this something must be causative most extensively and at the same time most excellently. In other words, God is that Reality (that Something or Someone) that creates ALL and rules over All, and does so in the BEST CONCEIVABLE MANNER.

## Divergent Views of God

Let us next examine some of the different possible ways of thinking about God. For, even if people agree on the basic point that "God" means *supreme being*, they may nonetheless hold to the most varied beliefs as to what precisely this supreme being is like. To facilitate our discussion, let us divide these differing conceptions of God into two broad categories, namely those which portray God as transcendent, and those depicting God as immanent. The central question at issue between these two categories of views is this: "How exactly does God stand in relation to the world?"

Among the views of God which have had the widest popular appeal are those which maintain that God is transcendent. Of course, the *word* "transcendent" is not commonly encountered in everyday conversation; it is used mainly by theologians and philosophers. However, the *idea* of transcendence is widely held--albeit sometimes only on a pre-reflective level. What is the significance of this notion?

The word "transcendent" is derived from the Latin words "trans" and "scandere," which mean *beyond* and *to climb*, respectively. When used in reference to God, the word "transcendent" signifies the radical separateness of God from the world. In other words, to say that God is transcendent amounts to the claim that God is entirely OTHER THAN the world. On this view, it is a mistake to believe that the Creator is in any way intimately tied to, or closely connected with, his creation, and so, it is, a fortiori, a mistake to say that God is strictly IDENTICAL with the world. If God is transcendent, if "he" is radically separate from the world, then we must understand there to be an unbridgeable gulf between the Creator and his creation; thus, the transcendence of God would render it absolutely impermissible for any creature ever to say "I am God" (or even "I am God-like"). If God is transcendent, then "he" stands immeasurably exalted above all "creatureliness."

According to the second broad category of views mentioned, God ought not to be thought of as radically separate from the world. That is, the various views of God subsumed under this category maintain that God is not altogether OTHER THAN the world, but rather is somehow INTIMATELY CONNECTED with the world, perhaps even identical with it. The word ordinarily used by philosophers and to convey this view of God is "immanent." It is important not to confuse this word with the similar-sounding "imminent" and "eminent." For the word "imminent" means impending; and "eminent" signifies outstanding or distinguished. The word "immanent," however, differs in meaning from both of these. It is derived from the Latin words "in" and "manere," which mean in and to dwell, respectively. Thus, the literal etymological meaning of "immanent" is in-dwelling. Accordingly, to say that God is immanent amounts to the claim that God in some sense actually dwells in the created world.

Now the most extreme interpretation of this "in-dwelling" of God is that of strict identity with the world. But, in any event, to view God as immanent is to regard "him" as somehow intimately connected with the world; it is to see the Creator as in some way intimately connected with the creation.

Let us turn, next, to a consideration of some of the particular conceptions of God that can be subsumed under each category. More specifically, we shall consider two pairs of such views. The first pair consists of two versions of what is termed "anthropomorphism"; these affirm the transcendence of God. The second pair comprises varieties of what is called "pantheism"; these belong to the category asserting the immanence of God. Let us begin with anthropomorphism.

"Anthropomorphism" is most concisely defined as the *ascription of human characteristics to God.* Its etymological components are the Greek words "anthropos," meaning *man,* and "morphe," which means *shape* or *form.* Thus, according to the anthropomorphic view of God, God must be conceived of as, in some sense, possessed of human form. But, in what sense precisely should we think of God as having human form? The problem here is to set forth an account of "having human form" which is worthy of God. How, in other words, must we understand "having human form," in order to insure the logical compatibility of that description with the lofty idea of the Supreme Being? Adherents of anthropomorphism tend to fall into two main classes, namely, those who take a *fundamentalist* stance, and those favoring a *spiritualist* interpretation. Let us briefly consider the two varieties of anthropomorphism in question.

The fundamentalist version of anthropomorphism assumes there to be no logical difficulty in the idea that God has a human form. We may take the adjective "fundamentalist" to imply insistence on a strictly literal understanding of the word "form" (i.e., "shape"). The fundamentalist anthropomorphist subscribes to the view that the Supreme Being literally has a human shape. Consequently, according to the fundamentalist variety of anthropomorphism, God, the Supreme Being, actually has a face, eyes, ears, nose, mouth, a complete set of four limbs, fingers, toes, and so on.

Those who think along such fundamentalist lines sometimes appeal for support to certain scriptural passages which--taken literally--clearly do impress upon the mind a picture of God as having a human shape. For example, toward the beginning of the book of Genesis in the Old Testament portion of the Bible we read the following: "And they heard the voice of the Lord God walking in the garden in the cool of the day: and Adam and his wife hid themselves from the presence of the Lord God amongst the trees of the garden." (Genesis 3:8)

In reading the above passage, we are naturally led to visualize God as walking, and to visualize God as walking is inseparably bound up with the thought that God actually has a human shape. There are many passages of this sort in the Bible, and also in the scriptures of the other major world religions. However, the question remains, "Is such a conception worthy of God?" Is it possible for God literally to have a human shape, and at the same time to be the supreme being? That is, is the literal possession of human shape logically compatible with divine supremacy? According to those who favor a purely spiritualist version of anthropomorphism, the answer to these questions is a definitive "no." Let us look more closely at this spiritualist view.

Since it is a variety of the anthropomorphic conception of God, the spiritualist view is fundamentally committed to the idea that ascribing human attributes to God is in some sense justified. On this view, God in a certain sense does have a human shape. However, the spiritualist differs from the fundamentalist by explicitly denying that the word "shape" can have literal applicability to God. Rather, for the spiritualist, to say that God has a human shape amounts to saying that God must be conceived of as possessing all of the spiritual attributes of humanity. The spiritual attributes of humanity are, broadly, the power of consciousness and the manifold expressions of this power in the various episodes of mental life. In other words, God--for the spiritualist--is possessed of such human characteristics as sight, hearing, imagination, intelligence, knowledge, love, compassion, kindliness, etc. Succinctly stated, God possesses consciousness, and all that the possession of consciousness implies. Moreover, the principal difference between God and human beings in this regard is that the spiritual attributes are perfect in God, whereas in humans these attributes are imperfect. But two further points should be emphasized.

The first point is that the spiritualist believes human consciousness to be possessed by God *in place of* literal human shape, not conjoined with such shape. According to this, we should not imagine God as in any sense having visualizable properties such as extension, figure, and space-occupancy. Rather, the spiritualist contends that God must be thought of in purely dynamic terms, i.e., exclusively in terms of power. We must conceive of God-on this view--as having power, *to the exclusion of* picturable qualities such as size, shape, and location. And we must understand that this power is specifically the power of CONSCIOUSNESS.

As to the second point, it is entirely possible for a spiritualist to admit the usefulness (or even the practical necessity) of forming pictures of God as in human shape. For instance, he might grant that it helps us during prayer or meditation to grasp more clearly the idea of the Supreme Being, if we hold in mind a visual image of God as literally in human form (e.g., as a King, seated on a throne in majestic surroundings, with hair and beard of brilliant whiteness, and with a countenance of dazzling splendor). But the spiritualist anthropomorphist is bound to maintain that such a picture is only an aid to understanding, and should not be taken as strictly accurate in reference to God.

The Christian who inclines toward this type of view will doubtless regard the following passages from the New Testament as scriptural confirmation for his position:

That which is born of the flesh is flesh: and that which is born of the Spirit is spirit. The wind bloweth where it listeth, and thou hearest the sound thereof, but canst not tell whence it cometh, and whither it goeth: so is every one that is born of the Spirit. (John 3:6-8)

But the hour cometh, and now is, when the true worshippers shall worship the Father in spirit and in truth: for the Father seeketh such to worship him. GOD IS A SPIRIT: and they that worship him must worship him in spirit and in truth. (John 4:23-24)

The scriptures of the other major religions also contain passages that seem to imply the conception of God as purely spiritual. For example, in Hinduism, God (i.e., Brahman) is explicitly described as *sachchidananda*. The Sanskrit word "sachchidananda" is a contraction formed from the words "sat," meaning *existence*, "chit," meaning *consciousness*, and "ananda," which means *joy*. The Hindu view of God as absolute Existence, Consciousness, and Joy is a thoroughly spiritual view of the Supreme Being; it includes no reference to anything corporeal (i.e., of a bodily nature).

So far, we have looked at conceptions of God which have in common the basic assumption that God is transcendent. That is, both the fundamentalist and spiritualist varieties of anthropomorphism conceive of God as standing apart from, or as wholly OTHER THAN, the world of created things. We shall next examine two views of the other sort we discussed, i.e., of the sort which affirms the immanence of the Supreme Being.

Among the views which assert God's immanence is the theory known as pantheism. The name "pantheism" is formed from the Greek words "pan" and "theos," which mean *all* and *God*, respectively. This view of God maintains exactly what its etymology suggests. That is, pantheism affirm that God is all, and consequently, that all is God. Two main forms of this theory can be distinguished, namely, the monist version of pantheism and its pluralist variety. We shall consider the monistic variety first.

To begin with, what is monism purely as such? Monism is the

metaphysical theory which maintains that ONE THING only exists. It affirms that, strictly speaking, there is only ONE BEING, but that an appearance of multiplicity arises from the fact that this ONE BEING has a great many "attributes" and "modes." The analogy of one ocean with many waves is sometimes invoked in order to clarify this. For, it is possible for us to think of an ocean as one, and at the same time to regard it as having infinitely many dispositions and episodes. Each wave in the ocean may be viewed as an episode manifesting a disposition of the ocean. Accordingly, the one BEING posited by monism may be thought of as having a relationship to its many attributes and modes which is similar to the relationship which obtains between the one ocean and its many wave-dispositions and wave-episodes. That is, the one BEING is like the ocean; the many attributes are like wave-dispositions; and the many modes are like wave-episodes.

Now, what we have designated as the monist variety of pantheism is based on the type of metaphysical view which we have just described. the monistic pantheist asserts that there exists in reality ONE THING only, and that this ONE THING is God. Thus, according to monistic pantheism, there is really nothing else apart from God. What seems to be something other than God is actually nothing but the very characteristics, states, and actions of God "himself." It follows that we--as many human beings--are not substantial entities, but rather merely passing events that happen to the one and only substantial entity, which is God. Such monistic thinking in regard to God has arisen to some extent within all of the major religious communities.

But, a pluralistic form of pantheism is also conceivable. Metaphysical pluralism is the theory that there exists a veritable multitude of substantial entities, i.e., of real beings or things. In other words, according to this view, the multitude which is evident all around us does not consist simply of events; the "many" are not merely passing accidents that *happen to* one and the same BEING, but rather each element in this multitude is a real substantial, thing that is itself possessed of attributes and capable of sustaining successive modes (i.e., successive *states* of itself). Now, what we have designated as the pluralist variety of pantheism presupposes the metaphysical theory we have just expounded. The pluralistic pantheist believes that there truly does exist a vast multitude of entities, and that the TOTALITY of these entities is what the word "God" refers to.

On this view, it is not the case that each individual being can rightly say "I am God." For, God is not identical with any one of these entities, but rather with the ENTIRE SET of entities, taken collectively. Accordingly, the most that a single being is entitled to say is: "I am a part of God." Moreover, although, prima facie, it is not logically necessitated by this view of God, the pluralistic pantheist is nonetheless very likely to regard the universe as fundamentally spiritual in nature. The idea that the universe is fundamentally spiritual in character implies that it is not to be thought of as a material system. It implies, in other words, that the universe should not be regarded as a multitude of *material* entities moving about and interacting in space, but rather as a great multitude of *spiritual* entities, each one of which is an unextended, figureless, indivisible and non-spatial *center*-of-consciousness.

The pluralistic pantheist typically takes the position that when the knower experiences the visible-tangible world, his own sense-experience interposes itself as a veil, and results in his mistakenly thinking that the exterior universe is a material system. But, according to this type of pluralistic position, the real exterior universe is *behind* the curtain of sensually experienced colors and forms; that is, it is wholly beyond the visual field of the individual knower. It is to this "real" universe that the pluralist refers when he claims that the universe is not a material system. To express this view metaphorically, the real universe wears a material mask, but its face is purely spiritual; it represents itself *in our sense experience* as a plurality of extended objects characterized by size and location, while in itself it consists exclusively of unextended, figureless, and non-spatial entities which are endowed with the power to manifest consciousness. Accordingly the pluralist variety of pantheism is typically conjoined with the view that the universe is nothing but a tremendous multitude of *spiritual beings*, and that God is simply this multitude of beings, taken as a totality.

The following is a passage from I Corinthians which a Christian pantheist--whether monist or pluralist--might appeal to as scriptural confirmation for this conception of God: "And when all things shall be subdued unto him, then shall the Son also himself be subject unto him that put all things under him, that God may be all in all." (I Corinthians 15:28) The same considerations apply to the following passage from the book of Acts: God "hath made of one blood all nations of men for to dwell on all the face of the earth, and hath determined the times before appointed, and the bounds of their habitation; That they should seek the Lord, if haply they might feel after him, and find him, though he be not far from every one of us: For in him we live, and move, and have our being...." (Acts 17:26-28) Similarly, pantheistically minded followers of the other major religions are able, in varying degrees, to find passages in their respective scriptures that appear to support this particular view of God.

## The Relative Merits of the Differing Views

So far, we have discussed four different theories as to what God is like. At this point let us take up the matter of appraising these differing views as to their plausibility. To what extent are the divergent conceptions that we have considered rationally justified? In the ensuing lines, I shall call attention to a certain logical difficulty encountered by all four of these views of God.

It should be noted at this juncture that all of the views which have been expounded are monotheistic in commitment, i.e., they all affirm the existence of ONE God only. The term "monotheism" is derived from the Greek words "monos" and "theos," which mean *one* and *God*, respectively. ("Polytheism," in contrast, signifies the belief in many gods.) Now, it is possible to distinguish three major varieties of monotheism, namely, the individualist, communitarian, and essentialist versions of monotheism. Let us first get clear concerning some key terms needed to make these distinctions, and then examine each form of monotheism, in turn.

To begin with, brief reference must be made to the ancient topic of "universals" and "particulars." Consider how the word "rose" leads us to think of entirely different things in the following two sentences: (1) A rose was taken from the king's garden; and (2) The rose is a beautiful flower. In sentence (1) the word "rose" evokes in us the thought of a specific thing, namely, the single rose that was picked. Using traditional philosophic terminology we would say that this single rose is a PARTICULAR. In sentence (2), however, the word "rose" leads us to think not of some specific single rose, but rather of that general something which permits us to say that each one of these single roses *is a rose*. In traditional nomenclature this general something is termed a UNIVERSAL.

In the above sentences the difference between the particular and the universal is brought out by use of the indefinite article "a" in the one case, and the definite article "the" in the other. In other words, the expression "a rose" conveys the thought of a PARTICULAR, while the expression "the rose" evokes the thought of a UNIVERSAL. But this is only one of numerous linguistic devices that can be used to underscore the difference between particulars and universals. One other linguistic device that can be used to indicate universality is that of adding the suffix "hood" to the basic noun. Thus, we could achieve similar results by employment of either "the rose" or "rose-hood." In other words, "rose-hood is that general something which justifies our application of the word "rose" to any one of a great many single entities. Moreover, just as we can distinguish between individual roses and rose-hood itself, we can make indefinitely many similar distinctions; thus, we have individual stones and stone-hood itself, individual trees and tree-hood itself, individual lions and lion-hood itself, and so on.

To reiterate, a particular is a single thing that can SHARE SOMETHING in common with many others, while a universal is what can BE SHARED in common by many single things. Now, throughout the history of thought the so-called "problem of universals" has been among the most perplexing that philosophers have had to address. What exactly are universals? What is their existential status? How precisely do they relate to particulars? There is still considerable uncertainty surrounding these and other questions regarding universals. Nonetheless, those philosophers who have thought most deeply about these matters are in agreement on at least one point, namely, that realism--in its main assumption--is a more plausible view that the other two broad positions commonly espoused. In other words, to claim that universals have no objective status--no status outside of the mind of the knower--is to embrace an implausible position. More specifically, on this view it is a mistake to say that only names are general (nominalism), and it is equally wrong to assert that only inner concepts are general (conceptualism). Those philosophers who have reflected most deeply on these questions are in agreement at least to the extent that they ascribe to universals some kind of objective status, i.e., some kind of standing external to the knowing subject. Moreover, that universals exist in some sense outside of the mind, in the "real" world, is the central contention of the various forms of realism. Of course, the above-mentioned agreement does not prove that realism is correct; nevertheless, the fact of this agreement should be kept in mind as we proceed with our discussion.

For present purposes, we can maintain neutrality vis a vis the numerous controversies surrounding the problem of universals. We need only make the assumption that some form of realism is the correct position to adopt.

There is one additional point that needs to be made before we begin to look at the several varieties of monotheism. I wish to call attention to a certain way of talking about the relation between universals and particulars. Let us use the fairly non-committal verb "to instantiate." We can say, then, that each single rose INSTANTIATES the rose, i.e, that it INSTANTIATES rose-hood. Moreover, we can say, generally, that each single thing, X, instantiates the X, i.e., instantiates X-hood. Thus, we have a means of referring to the relationship in question, without unduly committing ourselves as to the exact nature of that relationship.

We can now make use of the three words "particular," "universal," and "instantiate," in order to clarify the distinction between *individualist* monotheism, *communitarian* monotheism, and *essentialist* monotheism. Let us consider these three *seriatim*.

The individualist variety of monotheism is the view that there is one God only, and that this one God is a PARTICULAR. According to this form of monotheism, the one God is an individual, one being among many other beings. This is the popular (i.e., the most common) understanding of monotheism. Hence, there is no need to cite examples of this manner of thinking from the literature.

According to the communitarian version of monotheism, there is one God only and this one God is not a single particular, but rather ONE SET OF PARTICULARS, that is, one whole made up of many single beings or entities. In other words, the communitarian view maintains that the one God is a single COMMUNITY of individuals, not just one individual. This view is much less widely recognized as a possible form of monotheism than the former. Where it is thought of it is likely to be mistakenly classified as some form of polytheism. However, the temptation to regard this view as polytheistic should be resisted. The communitarian does not assert that each of the many members of the divine community is a God, but rather that this community *taken as a whole* is God. Moreover, this whole, as such, is not many, but rather one only. Although this is not a common form of monotheism, nonetheless, it has had and continues to have supporters. Among those who have articulated this view may be counted the philosopher and ethical reformer, Felix Adler. In his most important philosophic work, *An Ethical Philosophy of Life*, Adler expounds the communitarian position as follows:

> Have we then reinstated the idea of God as existent? Not the idea of God as an individual. We have on the contrary set aside that idea by affirming that manifoldness cannot be derived from unity, that the positing of plurality is just as much a primary function of the mind as the positing of unity. We have discarded the God-idea as the locus of unity, since the unity subsists in the relation of the units. Strictly speaking, we have replaced the God-idea by that of a universe of spiritual beings interacting in infinite harmony.[1]

This Adlerian conception of God as a single community of harmoniously related spiritual beings is typical of this form of monotheism. Moreover, the occasional use of expressions such as "Heaven" and "the Kingdom" as synonyms for "God" is very likely a reflection of the same type of thinking about God.

Finally, the essentialist variety of monotheism states that there is one God only, and that the one God is neither a single individual, nor a single community of individuals, but rather one UNIVERSAL, namely, the highest (or maximally inclusive) universal, which is that of BEING itself. That is to say, on the essentialist view, God is not *a* being, but rather *the* Being; He is not *a* person *among persons*, but rather He is *the* Person, one-and-absolutely-unique. In a word, this form of monotheism asserts that God is the one ESSENCE. Moreover, the essentialist typically believes that existence must be understood in spiritual terms. This would imply that "Being" is equivalent to "Spirit." The essentialist, therefore, favors the view that since Being *just is* Spirit, each individual being is *a* spirit, while God is *the* Spirit. We are all spirits, but God is Spirit-hood itself.

This essentialist view is more difficult to grasp than the other two versions of monotheism. Therefore, I will quote at length what is probably one of the earliest written expressions of this position. The following quotation is from the Upanishads, which are among the most authoritative scriptures of Hinduism. In this passage the wise man Uddalaka speaks to his son, Svetaketu, about the knowledge of Brahman (God), and about the relation of Brahman to his creatures:

When Svetaketu was twelve years old, his father Uddalaka said to him, "Svetaketu, you must now go to school and study. None of our family, my child, is ignorant of Brahman."
Thereupon Svetaketu went to a teacher and studied for twelve years. After committing to memory all the Vedas, he returned home full of pride in his learning.
His father, noticing the young man's conceit, said to him: "Svetaketu, have you asked for that knowledge by which we hear the unhearable, by which we perceive the unperceivable, by which we know the unknowable?"
"What is that knowledge, sir?" asked Svetaketu.
"My child, as by knowing one lump of clay, all things made of clay are known, the difference being only in name and arising from speech, and the truth being that all are clay; as by knowing a nugget of gold, all things made of gold are known, the difference being only in name and arising from speech, and the truth being that all are gold--exactly so is that knowledge, knowing which we know all."
"But surely those venerable teachers of mine are ignorant of this knowledge; for if they possessed it, they would have taught it to me. Do you therefore, sir, give me that knowledge?"
"Be it so," said Uddalaka, and continued thus:
"In the beginning there was Existence, One only, without a second. Some say that in the beginning there was nonexistence only, and that out of that the universe was born. But how could such a thing be? How could existence be born of non-existence? No, my son, in the beginning there was Existence alone--One only, without a second. He, the One, thought to himself: Let me be many, let me grow forth. Thus out of himself he projected the universe: and having projected out of himself the universe, he entered into every being and every thing. All that is has its self in him alone. He is the truth. He is the subtle *essence of all*. He is *the* Self. And that, Svetaketu, THAT ART THOU."
"Please, sir, tell me more about this Self."
"Be it so, my child:
"As the bees make honey by gathering juices from many flowering

plants and trees, and as these juices reduced to one honey do not know from what flowers they severally come, similarly, my son, all creatures, when they are merged in the one Existence, whether in dreamless sleep or in death, know nothing of their past or present state, because of the ignorance enveloping them--know not that they are merged in him and that from him they come."[2]

Notice how it is intimated in this passage that the relationship between God and his creatures is comparable to the relationship between clay itself and clay things, gold itself and gold nuggets, honey itself and honey drops. If we look into the full implications of these comparisons, we shall see that the essentialist character of the underlying view of God is undeniable. Consider, moreover, that God is explicitly referred to as EXISTENCE, and as the SELF. The original Sanskrit words translated here as *existence* and *self* are "sat" and "atman." The word "sat" can also be translated as Being, and "atman" is often rendered in English as Spirit. Finally, notice that this passage from the Upanishads actually describes God as the subtle ESSENCE of all.

It seems clear from the following quotation that the Christian philosopher St. Anselm also subscribed to the essentialist view of God:

For, since a man cannot be justness, but can possess justness, we do not conceive of a just man as *being* justness, but as possessing justness. Since, on the other hand, it cannot properly be said of the supreme Nature that it possesses justness, but that it is justness, when it is called just it is properly conceived of as *being* justness, but *not as possessing* justness. Hence, if, when it is said to be justness, it is not said of what character it is, but what it is, it follows that, when it is called just, it is not said of what character it is, but what it is.

Therefore, seeing that it is the same to say of the supreme Being, that it is just and that it is justness; and, when it is said that it is justness, it is nothing else than saying that it is just; it makes no difference whether it is said to be justness or to be just. Hence, when one is asked regarding the supreme Nature, what it is, the answer, *Just*, is not less fitting than the answer, *Justness*. Moreover, what we see to have been proved in the case of justness, the intellect is compelled to acknowledge as true of ALL

ATTRIBUTES which are similarly predicated of this supreme Nature.... It is, therefore,...supreme JUSTNESS, supreme WISDOM, supreme TRUTH, supreme GOODNESS, supreme GREATNESS, supreme BEAUTY, supreme IMMORTALITY, supreme INCORRUPTIBILITY, supreme IMMUTABILITY, supreme BLESSEDNESS, supreme ETERNITY, supreme POWER, supreme UNITY..., etc.[3]

A more recent statement of what appears to be basically the same position is found in the writings of the Christian theologian Paul Tillich. Consider the following passage from his work entitled *Systematic Theology*: "Thus the question of the existence of God can be neither asked nor answered. If asked, it is a question about that which by its very nature is above existence, and therefore the answer--whether negative or affirmative--implicitly denies the nature of God. It is as atheistic to affirm the existence of God as it is to deny it. God is being-itself, not a being."[4]

Let us return to the four views of God we discussed earlier. Specifically, let us turn our attention once again to fundamentalist anthropomorphism, spiritualist anthropomorphism, monistic pantheism, and pluralistic pantheism. What I would like to emphasize about these four positions is that they all have in common the assumption that God is a *particular*. For, both forms of anthropomorphism as well as the monistic variety of pantheism are subsumable under individualist monotheism; and consequently, all three of these views maintain that God is a single PARTICULAR. Moreover, the fourth view, viz., pluralistic pantheism, is subsumable under communitarian monotheism, and as such it, too, maintains that God is a PARTICULAR. However, to the pluralistic pantheist, God is not--strictly speaking--a *single* particular, but rather a *collective* particular. For, a community of particulars, considered as a whole, is no less a particular than are the members that make it up. Consequently, as stated above, all four of the views that we discussed earlier have in common the idea that God is a PARTICULAR.

But let us look more closely at the statement "God is a PARTICULAR." In attempting to unfold the implicit content of this statement, we can begin with the predicate nominative, "particular." Let it be noted first of all that "particular" implies *determined*. In other words, if God is a particular, then it necessarily follows that God is determined. For, every particular instantiates a universal, and is DETERMINED BY the universal which it instantiates.

What does it mean to say that a particular is determined by the universal which it instantiates? To say that a particular is determined by the universal which it instantiates amounts to saying that it is the universal that *makes (i.e., causes)* the particular *to be what it is.* This determination, this making-a-thing-to-be-what-it-is, should not be understood in terms of temporal sequence. It involves neither succession-of-events nor arising-and-perishing. Rather, this determining consists in a purely non-temporal, on-going relationship. A single rose, for example, is a particular. What is that by which it is determined? What is it that makes it to be what it is? What is it that makes it a rose? It is the universal which the rose instantiates that makes it a rose, that makes it to be what it is. Thus, the universal which the rose instantiates is that by which it is determined. Moreover, that the rose is determined follows necessarily from the very fact that it is a particular. For, every particular is necessarily determined by reason of the relationship which it bears to its universal.

Accordingly, if we claim that God is a particular, then we logically commit ourselves to the conclusion that--in the sense indicated above--God is determined.

Now, anything that is determined is necessarily causative to a lesser extent than that by which it is determined. Therefore, if God is a particular, it follows not only that God is determined by the universal which "he" instantiates, but also that God is causative to a LESSER EXTENT than the universal which "he" instantiates. Moreover, if God is causative to a lesser extent than the universal which "he" instantiates, then it cannot be the case that God is SUPERLATIVELY causative. In other words, if God were a particular, then God would necessarily instantiate a universal, and this universal would determine God, and would, consequently, be causative to a greater extent than God; and if this universal were causative to a GREATER extent than God, then God could not be *superlatively* causative.

But superlative causation--as we saw previously--is the core-content of the notion of supremacy. That is, if any given thing is--strictly speaking--SUPREME, then that thing must be superlatively causative.

Therefore, if God is not superlatively causative, then God is not strictly supreme. And to say that God is not supreme is equivalent to saying that the supreme Being is not supreme, for the very heart of the meaning of the word "God" is supreme being. Thus, we are led to a contradiction. That is, by unpacking the implicit content of our original statement "God is a particular," we are led to the discovery that this original statement is a disguised contradiction, and must be rejected.

We have already noted that the four views of God under consideration all have in common the assumption that God is a particular. Consequently, if the above line of reasoning is sound, then all four of these views must be rejected. For, it is possible to argue as follows: If one of these four views is correct, then God is a particular. But, it has been established that God is not a particular. Therefore, none of these four views of God is correct.

As regards a positive account of the nature of God, it seems clear that only some form of the essentialist view would be able to avoid the logical difficulties encountered by the individualist and communitarian positions we have been discussing. And, as indicated earlier, the essentialist conception of God requires that we think of God, not as a being among beings, but rather as Being itself, i.e., as the UNIVERSAL BEING. Moreover, since the essentialist view is ordinarily conjoined with a spiritual conception of Being, it typically maintains that God is not *a* spirit among spirits, but rather *the* Spirit itself, the UNIVERSAL SPIRIT. That is, it asserts that the universe is a vast multitude of individual spirits, and that the one God is "instantiated by," and therefore fully present within, each member of this spiritual community.

There are, moreover, additional considerations that can be adduced in support of the essentialist conception of God. If we look MORE DEEPLY into the concept of God itself, we shall uncover facts pertaining to this concept which render highly plausible the essentialist position. For, the concept of God implies the notion of superlative causation. Moreover, as previously noted, to be superlatively causative is--among other things--to be causative most EXTENSIVELY. But, what is it that is most extensively causative? In other words, what is it, ultimately, that causes each existing thing to be what it is, namely an existing thing? Is it not pure EXISTENCE itself, in the sense of the universal? Just as it may be said that it is rose-hood that causes each rose to be a rose, may it not similarly be said that it is being-hood, i.e., BEING itself, that causes each being to be a being?

Now, the various matters that we have been considering are doubtless of intrinsic philosophic interest. But we may well ask at this point: Of what importance are these various lines of thinking, from the standpoint of the masses of religious believers? Is any real benefit to be derived from gaining clarity on such matters? As the final endeavor of this chapter, I would like to call attention to one of the main practical ramifications of the concepts we have been discussing. In order to accomplish this, I shall first seek to underscore certain basic features of religion in general.

## Some Common Features of the Religions

Let us begin by noting that in every major religious tradition we encounter the idea that the prevailing condition of humanity is one of spiritual ignorance. The major religions do differ among themselves in the degree of emphasis they place on this point, and in how exactly they express it; nonetheless, we find common to all these traditions a teaching to the effect that we humans are ordinarily ignorant of God, that God, so to speak, is "hidden" from our gaze. According to this common teaching of the religions, we stand in relation to God similarly to how the blindfolded tent-dwellers stand in relations to the elephant. As the tent-dwellers are kept in ignorance of the elephant by their blindfolds, so also we are kept in ignorance of God by many successive veils that obstruct our spiritual vision. What exactly are these "veils" that prevent us from "seeing" God? This questions brings us to the next common feature of the religions to which I wish to refer.

Each of the major religions--in its own distinctive manner, and using its own distinctive terminology--teaches that the cause of our spiritual ignorance comes in the last analysis to one thing only, specifically what can be termed *misguided attachment*. The many successive "veils" that keep us in ignorance of God are simply the numerous forms of misguided attachment established within us as enduring dispositions. Let us look more deeply into this notion of misguided attachment.

What we have designated here as misguided attachment has two main components, namely, *selfishness* and *worldliness*. To be selfish is to love oneself exclusively and excessively. To love oneself exclusively is, fundamentally, to be disposed to take delight in one's own reality and well-being, without at the same time being disposed to take delight in the reality and well-being of others. Moreover, to love oneself excessively is, fundamentally, to be disposed to take delight in one's own reality and well-being in a degree that is not justified by their actual value.

The other component of misguided attachment is what we have called worldliness. As commonly employed, the term "worldliness" involves a reference to the world in a restricted sense of the word "world"; the reference is to this world, i.e., to the visible-tangible world. Thus, to be worldly is to love this world exclusively and excessively. To love this world exclusively is, fundamentally, to be disposed to take delight in it, without at the same time being disposed to take delight in the thought of another and better world. Hence, worldliness necessarily involves a failure to acknowledge the existence of any other world apart from this visible-tangible world. And to love this world excessively is, fundamentally, to be disposed to take delight in it to an extent that is not justified by its actual value.

Misguided attachment is a kind of psychological bondage, in which one's emotional state is dependent on the constantly changing things and circumstances of this visible-tangible world. It is, thus, a condition in which our peace of mind and our happiness are at the mercy of life's vicissitudes; it is a condition in which we are incapable of standing firm in the face of alternating pleasure and pain, good fortune and ill fortune, praise and condemnation, and good treatment and ill treatment at the hands of others.

To reiterate, the major religions share in common the teaching that the various forms of selfishness and worldliness constitute the veils that prevent us from "seeing" God. In a word, it is misguided attachment that keeps us ignorant of God.

There is a third common feature of the religions that needs to be noted. The major religions all agree that the central goal of the religious life is the knowledge of God, or in other words, to be released from the prevailing state of spiritual ignorance. Just as each of the blindfolded tent-dwellers had the possibility of arriving at a knowledge of the elephant, so also all human beings can be delivered from their state of spiritual ignorance, and attain a knowledge of God.

Finally, the fourth common teaching is this: The primary means by which the goal of spiritual knowledge can be attained is religious detachment. That is to say, by establishing and gradually strengthening within ourselves the attitude of religious detachment, we will be able to come closer and closer to the goal of spiritual knowledge, until at last we achieve the "vision" of God. This process of cultivating detachment may be compared to removing successively numerous blindfolds from the eyes of a tent-dweller, so that he ultimately is enabled to see the elephant. But, what exactly is this religious detachment?

To answer the above question, we may simply "reverse" the statements previously made in connection with attachment, for "detachment" has the opposite meaning. Thus, religious detachment also has two main components, namely, *unselfishness* and *spirituality*. To be unselfish is to love humanity with an all-inclusive and value-commensurate love. To love humanity allinclusively is, fundamentally, to be disposed to take delight in the reality and well-being of all persons (others equally with oneself) purely by reason of their person-hood as such. To love humanity value-commensurately is, fundamentally, to be disposed to take delight in the reality and well-being of persons in that sublime degree that is justified by the actual worth that is indefeasibly bound up with person-hood as such.

The other component of religious detachment is spirituality, or, less ambiguously, the quality of being spiritually-MINDED, i.e., mindful of Spirit. To be spiritual, that is to say, spiritually-minded, is to love the "world" all-inclusively and value-commensurately. Loving the world all-inclusively consists in not confining one's love to this visible-tangible world, but rather extending it to embrace that other "higher" world posited by the religions. That is, our love for the world is all-inclusive insofar as we are disposed to take delight both in the things that make up its visible-tangible division, and in the thought of its higher spiritual division. And to love the world value-commensurately is to be disposed to take delight in its visible-tangible division, and in its higher spiritual division to a degree that is in conformity with their actual worth. In particular, it involves assigning the lesser degree of value to this visible-tangible portion, and the greater degree of value to that unseen or supersensible portion.

Religious detachment is a kind of psychological freedom in which one's emotional state is not under the control of the ever-fluctuating exterior world. To make progress in religious detachment is to grow in one's ability to pass through the vicissitudes of life unruffled. To the extent that our peace of mind and happiness are no longer at the mercy of fleeting events, transitory circumstances, and the merely accidental characteristics of our fellow human beings, to that extent we have succeeded in cultivating the attitude of religious detachment. And, as stated previously, the various religions are agreed on the point that growing in such detachment is equivalent to advancing toward the knowledge of God.

To summarize, I have suggested that the major religions are in agreement on the following points: (1) The "human" condition is one of ignorance of God; (2) The cause of this ignorance is misguided attachment; (3) The goal of the religious life is the knowledge of God; and (4) The means by which this goal may be attained is the cultivation of religious detachment.

### Practical Import

It was suggested earlier that our various reflections concerning God are of definite practical importance for the religious life. I shall appeal to the several points just made concerning religion in general in an effort to support this suggestion. However, before doing this, let us examine a series of quotations from different religious traditions. For, if we think into the deeper meaning of these quotations, they will be seen to confirm that the four teachings just enumerated are in fact common to the major religions.

In the *Bhagavad Gita* of Hinduism we read:

Hear now how he then reaches Brahman, the highest vision of Light. When the vision of reason is clear, and in steadiness the soul is in harmony; when the world of sound and other senses is gone, and the spirit has risen above passion and hate; when a man dwells in the solitude of silence, and meditation and contemplation are ever with him; when too much food does not disturb his health, and his thoughts and words and body are in peace; when freedom from passion is his constant will; and his selfishness and violence and pride are gone; when lust and anger and greediness are no more, and he is free from the thought "this is mine"; then this man has risen on the mountain of the Highest:  he is worthy to be one with Brahman, with God.  He is one with Brahman, with God, and beyond grief and desire his soul is in peace.  His love is one for all creation.[5]

The following is from the Buddhist scripture entitled *The Dhammapada*:

The deluded, imagining trivial things to be vital to life, follow their vain fancies and never attain the highest knowledge.  But the wise, knowing what is trivial and what is vital, set their thought on the supreme goal and attain the highest knowledge.  As rain seeps through an ill-thatched hut, passion will seep through an untrained mind.  As rain cannot seep through a well-thatched hut, passion cannot seep through a well-trained mind.  Those who are selfish suffer here and hereafter; they suffer in both worlds from the results of their own actions.  But those who are selfless rejoice here and rejoice hereafter.  They rejoice in both worlds from the results of their own actions.[6]

In the Gospel of Matthew, in response to the pharisaic lawyer who had asked, "Master, which is the great commandment of the law?" Jesus declared:

Thou shalt love the Lord thy God with all thy heart, and with all thy soul, and with all thy mind.  This is the first and great commandment.  And the second is like unto it, Thou shalt love thy neighbor as thyself.  On these two commandments hang the law and the prophets.[7]

As a final illustration, consider the following passage from the writings of Abdu'l-Baha, one of the central figures of the Baha'i Faith:

If thou seekest to be intoxicated with the cup of the Most Mighty Gift, cut thyself from the world and be quit of self and desire.  Exert thyself night and day until spiritual powers may penetrate thy heart and soul.  Abandon the body and the material, until the merciful powers may become manifest; because not until the soil is become pure will it develop through the heavenly bounty; not until the heart is purified will the radiance of the Sun of Truth shine therein. I beg of God that thou wilt day by day increase the purity of thy heart, the cheerfulness of thy soul, the light of thy insight and the search for Truth.[8]

Now, in keeping with the foregoing discussion, we can affirm that whatever assists us to develop religious detachment has practical utility for the religious life. Thus, the chief practical importance of the sort of God-centered thinking we have engaged in is this: Such thinking can contribute to the attainment of religious detachment. For the more we reflect on God, the more clearly we see that the very concept of God logically entails the idea of the absolute ASCENDANCY OF GOODNESS. In other words, the very notion of God is inseparably bound up with the idea that all things are in subjection to the governing influence of Goodness, i.e., that all is determined and controlled by Goodness. And to become ever more deeply aware of this all-encompassing Ascendancy of Goodness is conducive to the attainment of religious detachment.

Moreover, in this connection, it does not matter whether one adopts an anthropomorphic, pantheist, or essentialist view of God, since all of these differing views of God have in common the one thing which is crucial for developing religious detachment. This common element is the idea of divine supremacy itself. For, the very notion of the Supreme Being, as such, leads to progressively greater degrees of religious detachment, on condition that we exert ourselves to grasp ever more deeply the implicit content of this notion. Furthermore--and this is my main point--the idea of the Supreme Being facilitates our growth in detachment equally well, whether we imagine this Supreme Being to be in HUMAN SHAPE (anthropomorphism), IDENTICAL WITH ALL (pantheism), or the one ESSENCE of all (Essentialism).

Let me try to state this a bit more explicitly. The notion of a supreme being leads inexorably to the idea of the absolute Ascendancy of Goodness, i.e., the idea that it is Goodness that determines all things. And on the basis of this idea, we can build ourselves up in an unshakably positive outlook upon the whole of existence. For, as noted earlier, the notion of a supreme being entails the idea of a Something or Someone that is causative most extensively and most excellently; in other words, the supreme being is necessarily both creator of all and ruler over all. And this leads us to the thought that all things, events, and circumstances--that are genuinely within the sphere of reality--are the very BEST conceivable. This, then, is the significance of talking about the Ascendancy of Goodness. Moreover, to immerse ourselves ever more deeply in this thought of the Ascendancy of Goodness just is to grow in that thoroughly positive outlook on existence which constitutes true religious detachment.

Clearly, then, God-centered reflection of the sort that we have engaged in can contribute to the development of religious detachment. And, as we have noted, whatever contributes to the development of religious detachment has practical importance for the religious life. Consequently, such God-centered reflection as we have engaged in, and the increased clarity to which it leads, are of practical significance for the religious life. Indeed, growth in detachment is among the chief benefits to be derived from gaining greater clarity on the concept of God and its implications.

*Notes*

[1]Felix Adler, *An Ethical Philosophy of Life* (New York: Ethica Press, 1986), p. 126.
[2]*The Upanishads*, tr. Prabhavananda (Hollywood: Vedanta Press, 1971), pp. 108-110. (Italics added.)
[3]St. Anselm, *Basic Writings* (La Salle, IL: Open Court Publishing, 1962), pp. 111-112. (Emphasis added.)
[4]Paul Tillich, *Systematic Theology* (Chicago: University of Chicago Press), p. 237.
[5]*The Bhagavad Gita*, tr. J. Mascaro (Baltimore: Penguin Books, 1962), pp. 119-120.
[6]*The Dhammapada*, tr. E. Easwaran (Berkeley: Nilgiri Press, 1986), p. 79.
[7]Matthew 22:37-40.
[8]*Baha'i World Faith* (Wilmette, IL: Baha'i Publishing Trust, 1976), p. 362.

CHAPTER FOUR:


PROVING THAT GOD EXISTS

CHAPTER FOUR:  Proving that God Exists

In the previous chapter, we sought to gain increased clarity in connection with the *concept* of God.  But what rational considerations, if any, can be adduced to support the claim that something conforming to this concept *actually exists*?  How can we *prove* that God exists?

In the present chapter, I would like for us to focus on certain classic theistic proofs.  In using the designation "classic theistic proofs," I refer to those attempts at proving God's existence which have been most influential historically, and most widely discussed by philosophers.  Let us begin with what is called the "ontological argument" for God's existence.

The Ontological Argument

The philosopher to whom credit is ordinarily given for having first formulated the ontological argument is St. Anselm of Canterbury (A.D. 1033-1109).  Anselm's argument was first set forth in a short work entitled *Proslogium* (i.e., *A Discourse*).  Throughout the long period since this argument was first put forward by Anselm, discussions of it have tended to focus on Chapter II of the *Proslogium*, especially the last two paragraphs of Chapter II. In that chapter, having defined "God" as *that-than-which-nothing-greater-can-be-conceived*, Anselm states the following:

> Hence, even the fool is convinced that something exists in the understanding, at least, than which nothing greater can be conceived. For, when he hears this, he understands it. And whatever is understood, exists in the understanding. And assuredly that, than which nothing greater can be conceived, cannot exist in the understanding alone. For, suppose it exists in the understanding alone: then it can be conceived to exist in reality; which is greater.
>
> Therefore, if that, than which nothing greater can be conceived, exists in the understanding alone, the very being, than which nothing greater can be conceived, is one, than which a greater can be conceived. But obviously this is impossible. Hence, there is no doubt that there exists a being, than which nothing greater can be conceived, and it exists both in the understanding and in reality.[1]

In keeping with how it is understood by the majority of commentators, the above quotation could be reconstructed as follows:

PART I
(1) Premise:  If that-than-which-nothing-greater-can-be-conceived exists in THOUGHT ONLY, then that-than-which-nothing-greater-can-be-conceived IS NOT that-than-which-nothing-greater-can-be-conceived, for it is always possible to conceive of something greater than what exists in thought only.
(2) Premise:  But, it is obviously a mistake to say that that-than-which-nothing-greater-can-be-conceived IS NOT that-than-which-nothing-greater-can-be-conceived, for this would be equivalent to saying that something IS NOT what it IS.
CONCLUSION:  Therefore, it is a mistake to say that that-than-which-nothing greater-can-be-conceived exists in THOUGHT ONLY.
Part II

(1)Premise:      That-than-which-nothing-greater-   can-be-conceived either exists in THOUGHT ONLY, or it exists both in thought and IN REALITY.
(2) Premise:  As established in PART I above, it is a mistake to say that   that-than-which-nothing-greater-can-be-conceived   exists   in THOUGHT ONLY.
CONCLUSION:         Therefore,        that-than-which-nothing-greater-can-be-conceived exists both in thought and IN REALITY.

Now, if the interpretation expressed in this reconstruction is correct, then it is abundantly clear why the majority of philosophers have always imagined that refuting the ontological argument is an altogether easy task. Throughout the centuries since the ontological argument was first formulated, the main objection which its many critics have always tended to raise is essentially this: Anselm is guilty of circular reasoning. The 19th century German philosopher Arthur Schopenhauer expresses this traditional objection by the use of a comparison. According to Schopenhauer, anyone who tries to prove God's existence by means of the ontological argument is comparable to the "magician" who pulls a rabbit out of his hat, as if miraculously. Schopenhauer's point is that the "magician" must first of all *put the rabbit into his hat furtively* (i.e., without allowing his audience to observe what he does), in order to be able to take it out of his hat afterwards. According to Schopenhauer, something similar happens in connection with the ontological argument; he suggests that the key premise of this argument may be likened to the magician's hat, while the statement "God exists" is like the rabbit which the magician pulls out of the hat. In other words, the objection is that Anselm commits the fallacy of begging the question, since he first surreptitiously slips "God exists" into his main premise, and subsequently presents this same proposition as the *conclusion* of his argument.

This "traditional criticism" of the ontological argument was first set forth in writing by Gaunilon of Marmoutier, a  French monk who lived contemporaneously with Anselm.  In order to obtain further clarity concerning the so-called traditional criticism, let us consider the very first statement of this objection, which   appears   in   the   written   reply   of Gaunilon to Anselm's *Proslogium*. Gaunilon's reply bears the title *In Behalf of the Fool*, which alludes to the "fool" (mentioned in the biblical book of Psalms) who says in his heart "There is no God." Having asked Anselm   to   form   the   conception   of   an   *ISLAND-than-which-a-greater-*

*cannot-be-conceived*, Gaunilon states his objection as follows:

> Now if some one should tell me that there is such an island, I should easily understand his words, in which there is no difficulty. But suppose that he went on to say, as if by a logical inference: "You can no longer doubt that this island which is more excellent than all lands exists somewhere, since you have no doubt that it is in your understanding. And since it is more excellent not to be in the understanding alone, but to exist both in the understanding and in reality, for this reason it must exist. For if it does not exist, any land which really exists will be more excellent than it; and so the island already understood by you to be more excellent will not be more excellent."

> If a man should try to prove to me by such reasoning that this island truly exists and that its existence should no longer be doubted, either I should believe that he was jesting, or I know not which I ought to regard as the greater fool: myself, supposing that I should allow this proof; or him, if he should suppose that he had established with any certainty the existence of this island. For he ought to show first that the hypothetical excellence of this island exists as a real and indubitable fact, and in no wise as any unreal object, or one whose existence is uncertain, in my understanding.[2]

If we employ the following reconstruction of Gaunilon's objection, its full significance can readily be seen:

> (1) Premise: If the ontological argument does prove the existence of God, then it is possible--by parity of reasoning--to prove the existence of a host of other things which obviously do not exist, e.g., an island-than-which-a-greater-cannot-be-conceived.
> (2) Premise: But it certainly is not possible--by parity of reasoning--to prove the existence of such a host of other things.
> CONCLUSION: Therefore, the ontological argument does not prove the existence of God.

Now, the question that I wish to raise is this: Is the traditional criticism of the ontological argument a legitimate objection, that is, does it really succeed in refuting Anselm's argument? In attempting to arrive at an answer to this question, let us begin by noting that a basic presupposition underlying Anselm's argument is that set forth in the following statement: That-than-which-nothing-greater-can-be-conceived exists in the understanding (i.e., in thought). The truth of this statement is assumed to be obvious, and entirely uncontroversial. But, what we need to consider concerning this statement is that it is characterized by a certain ambiguity. For, to say that that-than-which-nothing-greater-can-be-conceived exists in the understanding could be taken to mean either: (A) The CONCEPT-OF-that-than-which-nothing-greater-can-be-conceived exists in the understanding, or (B) The THING-ITSELF-than-which-nothing-greater-can-be-conceived exists in the understanding. Let us designate the two possibilities as Interpretation A, and Interpretation B, respectively. Now, which of the two is the correct interpretation?

Insofar as our reconstruction assumes it to be JUST OBVIOUS that that-than-which-nothing-greater-can- be-conceived exists in the understanding, we are forced to take Interpretation A as the one which Anselm intended. For, only on this interpretation is it plausible to maintain that the presupposition in question is *just obvious.* The CONCEPT-OF-that-than-which-nothing-greater-can-be-conceived is simply the *idea or thought* of the thing, and not the thing itself. And it would be universally admitted as true that the *idea* of that-than-which-nothing-greater- can-be-conceived exists in the understanding of each person who hears and attends to the meaning of the phrase "that than which nothing greater can be conceived." However, on the alternative interpretation, i.e., Interpretation B, it would surely *not* be just obvious that that-than-which-nothing-greater-can-be-conceived exists in the understanding. On the contrary, the claim that the THING ITSELF exists in the understanding whenever it is inwardly contemplated, or thought about, would appear to be highly doubtful. Consequently, to reiterate, it is certain that we must take Interpretation A as the one intended, insofar as the presupposition under consideration is to be regarded as uncontroversially true.

Now, let us look once again at the reconstruction itself. The first premise in PART I of this reconstruction makes the following assertion: If that-than-which-nothing-greater-can-be-conceived exists in THOUGHT ONLY, then that-than-which-nothing-greater- can-be-conceived IS NOT that-than-which-nothing-greater-can-be-conceived, for it is always possible to conceive of something greater than what exists in thought only. In order for this premise of the reconstruction to be seen as plausible, we must take Interpretation B as the one intended. For, clearly, it is not the case that whatever we may say concerning the CONCEPT of a thing, we must also be able to say concerning the THING ITSELF. Thus, from the fact that we cannot conceive of anything greater than some given thing, it does not follow that we cannot conceive of anything greater than the CONCEPT of that thing. We may say, for instance, that water is a wet THING, but is would not follow from this that the CONCEPT (i.e., the *idea* or *thought*) of water is a wet CONCEPT; similarly, we may say that the sun is a hot THING, but it would not follow from this that the CONCEPT of the sun is a hot CONCEPT. More specifically, even though it certainly must be granted that it is impossible to conceive of something *greater than* the THING-ITSELF-than-which-nothing-greater-can-conceived, it does not follow from this that it is impossible to conceive of something greater than the CONCEPT-OF-that-than-which-nothing-greater-can-be--conceived. In other words, we must understand the afore-mentioned presupposition in a sense such that we may take the reconstruction to be saying: The THING-ITSELF-than-which-nothing-greater-can-be-conceived could not possibly exist in thought only, but rather, by its very nature, would have to exist both in thought and in reality.

Now, let us keep in mind that we are considering a certain presupposition of Anselm's argument, as reconstructed at the beginning of this chapter, namely this:  That-than-which-nothing-greater-can-be-conceived exists in the understanding. The main point which I just sought to emphasize is that premise (1) of PART I makes this presupposition in the sense of Interpretation B. In other words, this premise of the reconstruction forces us to take the statement "That-than-which-nothing-greater-can-be-conceived  exists  in   the understanding" as meaning: *The THING-ITSELF-than-which-nothing-greater-can-be-conceived exists in the understanding.* Moreover, from what has been said, it  would appear that the traditional criticism does constitute a legitimate objection to Anselm's argument.  For, it is clear that this  argument--as reconstructed at the outset--simply *assumes* what it is supposed to *prove*, i.e., it begs the question.  To be more explicit, premise (1) of PART I of the reconstruction already assumes that the THING-ITSELF-than-which-nothing-greater-can-be-conceived   EXISTS, and this is the very conclusion which the argument ultimately aims to establish.

The foregoing considerations also make it clear that Anselm's argument (as reconstructed) commits the fallacy of equivocation. For, on the one hand, Interpretation A must be implicitly invoked, in order to gain assent to the non-controversial character of the argument's basic presupposition; while, on the other hand, Interpretation B must be taken, in order to render plausible the main conditional premise by means of which the argument arrives at its final conclusion. This illicit shift in the meaning assigned to "That-than-which-nothing-greater-can-be-conceived exists in the understanding" is a fundamental flaw in Anselm's argument, as it is ordinarily understood. There can be no doubt but that, if Anselm really intended to argue what is set forth in the earlier reconstruction, then he was seriously confused as regards the distinction between the CONCEPT of a thing and the THING ITSELF which corresponds to that concept. The upshot of these remarks is that the ontological argument--as reconstructed--does not succeed in establishing that God exists.

Let us again focus on the reconstruction set forth at the outset of this chapter. To facilitate our discussion, we may refer to it as the "common reconstruction." As stated previously, the common reconstruction represents the usual understanding of what Anselm intended to argue in Chapter II of the *Proslogium*. But, is this what Anselm actually intended to argue? I wish to suggest that the answer to this questions is "no." I shall attempt to show that the traditional criticism, which we have been discussing, is in reality directed against a "straw man." The locution "straw man fallacy" refers to any instance of misguided reasoning which undertakes to attack some particular position, but which in actuality is directed against some OTHER position, that is, against a distortion of the real target-position (which distortion is more or less similar to it, but more vulnerable to attack). I submit that what we actually saw in the foregoing discussion is that the traditional criticism is successful insofar as it is directed against what in fact is a "distortion" of the ontological argument. However, the traditional criticism does not constitute a decisive refutation of the argument which Anselm actually put forward.

But, if the usual interpretation of Chapter II is a distortion, then what exactly did Anselm intend to argue in that chapter? I wish to assert that the argument which Anselm really intended to advance is the following:

PART I

(1) Premise: If the CONCEPT of that-than-which-nothing-greater-can-be-conceived were the CONCEPT of something which existed in THOUGHT ONLY, then the CONCEPT of that-than-which--nothing-greater-can-be-conceived would not be the CONCEPT of that-than-which-nothing-greater-can-be-conceived   for   the CONCEPT of something which exists in THOUGHT ONLY is the CONCEPT of something than which it is possible to conceive of something greater.

(2) Premise:   But, it is obviously a mistake to say that the CONCEPT of that-than-which-nothing- greater-can-be-conceived is not the CONCEPT of that-than-which-nothing-greater-can-be-conceived, for that would be equivalent to saying that this CONCEPT is *not* what it *is*.

CONCLUSION:   Therefore, it is a mistake to say that the CONCEPT of that-than-which-nothing- greater-can-be-conceived is the CONCEPT of something that exists in THOUGHT ONLY.

PART II

(1) Premise:   The CONCEPT of that-than-which-nothing-greater-can-be-conceived is either the CONCEPT of something which exists in THOUGHT ONLY, or it is the CONCEPT of something which exists BOTH in thought and IN REALITY.

(2) Premise:   As established in PART I above, it is a mistake to say that the CONCEPT of that-than-which-nothing-greater-can-be-conceived is the CONCEPT of something which exists in THOUGHT ONLY.

CONCLUSION: Therefore, the CONCEPT of that-than-which-nothing-greater-can-be-conceived is the CONCEPT of something which exists BOTH in thought and IN REALITY.

That this alternative reconstruction is the correct way in which to look at Chapter II is made evident by an examination of other passages from Anselm's writings in which he presents the ontological argument. For, Chapter II is only one of several places where Anselm states his argument.   Consider, for instance, the following passage from Anselm's *Apologium*, which he wrote in response to the objections raised by Gaunilon's *In Behalf of the Fool*:

Moreover, it is evident that in the same way it is possible to conceive of and understand a being whose non-existence is impossible; but he who conceives of this conceives of a greater being than one whose non-existence is possible. Hence, when a being than which a greater is inconceivable is conceived, if it is a being whose nonexistence is possible that is conceived, it is not a being than which a greater cannot be conceived. But an object cannot be at once conceived and not conceived. Hence he who *conceives of* a being than which a greater is inconceivable, does not *conceive of* that whose non-existence is possible, but of that whose non--existence is impossible. Therefore, what he conceives of must exist; *for anything whose non-existence is possible, is not that of which he conceives.*[3]

This quotation from the *Apologium* strongly suggests that the alternative reconstruction presented above constitutes an accurate account of the argument that Anselm had in mind in Chapter II of the *Proslogium*. Thus, the usual rabbit-in-the-hat type of objection that tends to be levelled against Anselm does not refute the argument which he actually set forth, but, as previously suggested, is only applicable against a distortion of that argument. It must, however, be conceded that the formulation given in Chapter II of the *Proslogium*, and re-appearing less obscurely in the *Apologium*, is elliptical and indirect. Anselm states the main point of the ontological argument in a far more explicit manner in Chapters III and IV of the *Proslogium*:

> For, it is possible to conceive of a being which cannot be conceived not to exist; and this is greater than one which can be conceived not to exist. Hence, if that, than which nothing greater can be conceived, can be conceived not to exist, it is not that, than which nothing greater can be conceived. But this is an irreconcilable contradiction. There is, then, so truly a being than which nothing greater can be conceived to exist, that it cannot even be conceived not to exist; and this being thou art, O Lord, our God.[4]
> So, then, no one who understands what God is can conceive that God does not exist; although he says these words in his heart, either without any, or with some foreign, signification. For, God is that than which a greater cannot be conceived. And he who thoroughly understands this, assuredly understands that this being so truly exists, that not even in concept can it be non-existent. Therefore, he who understands that God so exists, cannot conceive

that he does not exist.[5]

The basic line of argumentation advanced in the above quotations could be re-worded as follows:

PART I
(1) Premise:    If the very concept of that-than-which-nothing-greater-can-be-conceived includes the notion of existence, then that-than-which nothing-greater-can-be-conceived does exist.
(2) Premise:  The very concept of that-than-which-nothing-greater-can-be-conceived does in fact include the notion of existence.
CONCLUSION:  Therefore,that-than-which-nothing-greater-can-be-conceived does exist.
PART II
(1) Premise:  By the word "God" is simply meant *that-than-which-nothing-greater-can-be-conceived.*
(2)    Premise:       As     established    in    PART    I    above, that-than-which-nothing-greater-can-be-conceived does exist.
CONCLUSION:  Therefore, God does exist.

Thus, the central idea of the ontological argument is that the statement "God exists" is logically necessary. Alternatively, the point could be put by saying that the statement "God does not exist" is logically self-contradictory. In other words, the statement "God is existent" is assumed to be similar to such statements as "Bachelors are single," "Widows are females," and "Fathers are parents"; whereas, the statement "God is non-existent" is taken to be comparable to such statements as "Bachelors are not single," Widows are not females," and "Fathers are not parents." What is noteworthy about the former three statements is the fact that the subject-concept of each *contains*, as an element within itself, the very idea that is expressed in its predicate; but, in each of the latter three statements the subject-concept *excludes* the predicate-idea, as something incompatible with itself.

Now, both sets of statements mentioned above have a character such that they can be determined to be true or false--as the case may be--purely by means of an examination of the concepts involved; that is, their truth or falsity may be ascertained simply by means of thinking out the logical implications of the subject-concepts which they contain. The ontological argument maintains that the statement "God exists" has this same character, namely a character such that its truth can actually be "seen," as the result of a careful and sustained consideration of the inner content of the concept of God. But, let us be altogether clear on this point. The ontological argument assumes that the concept of God has a *logically necessary* connection with the notion of existence, not merely a contingent connection. Anselm believed that there is no need for the idea of existence to be artificially attached, or added, to the concept of God; rather, he supposed that the notion of existence is something that we actually DISCOVER in the course of unpacking the *natural* content of the concept of God.

To illustrate the distinction between a logically necessary connection and a merely contingent connection, consider the following sentences: (1) Blue things are *extended* things, and (2) Circular lines are *endless* lines. With respect to sentence (1), it should be noted that the idea of blue-ness and that of extension are TWO distinct concepts; nevertheless, there is no need for the idea of extension to be artificially attached, or added, to the concept of blue-ness. Rather, the idea of extension is something which we actually DISCOVER in the course of unfolding the implications of the concept of blue-ness. Being *blue* necessitates being *extended*, and it is impossible even to conceive of something that is blue, but nonetheless unextended. Thus, we may say that the concept of that-which-is-blue has a *logically necessary* connection with the idea of that-which-is-extended.

But there are certainly many other ideas with which the concept of that-which-is-blue has no such necessary connection. If, for example, we think of some particular blue thing which is cylinder-shaped, it is clear that the connection between the idea of blue-ness and that of cylindricality is only a *contingent* connection; for, there is nothing in the nature of blue-ness, as such, which necessitates cylindricality.

Similar things may be said with regard to sentence (2) above as were just stated concerning sentence (1). The concept of that-which-is-circular has a *logically necessary* connection with the idea of that-which-is-endless. We unavoidably encounter, or come up against, the idea of endlessness, if we persist in unfolding the implications of the concept of circularity. There is no need to tie together these two concepts artificially; rather, we actually DISCOVER a connection between the two, which *already* existed prior to the outset of this process of "unfolding."

Now, in a critical assessment of the ontological argument, the most important question to ask would be: Does the very *concept* of God--when it is sufficiently clearly apprehended or understood--show in a decisive way that God in fact does exist? In other words, if we set about to unfold the inner implications of the concept of that-than-which-nothing-greater-can-beconceived, will such a process of "unfolding" actually lead us to the realization or insight that that-than-which-nothing-greater-can-be-conceived does exist? Anselm, of course, would answer this question in the affirmative. Moreover, in the *Apologium* he sought to defend this affirmative answer. In concluding our consideration of the ontological argument, let us take a brief look at one facet of his attempted defense:

> If it should be said that a being than which a greater cannot be conceived has no real existence, or that it is possible that it does not exist, or even that it can be conceived not to exist, such an assertion can easily be refuted. For the non-existence of what does not exist is possible, and that whose non-existence is possible can be conceived not to exist. But whatever can be conceived not to exist, if it exists, is not a being than which a greater cannot be conceived; but if it does not exist, it would not, even if it existed, be a being than which a greater cannot be conceived. But it cannot be said that a being than which a greater is inconceivable, if it exists, is not a being than which a greater is inconceivable; or that if it existed, it would not be a being than which a greater is inconceivable.

> It is evident, then, that neither is it non-existent, nor is it possible that it does not exist, nor can it be conceived not to exist. For otherwise, if it exists, it is not that which it is said to be in the hypothesis; and if it existed, it would not be what it is said to be in hypothesis.[6]

In the above quotation, Anselm actually states several distinct arguments simultaneously. I wish to separate-out one of these distinct lines of argumentation. Let us employ the following reconstruction for that purpose:

PART I
(1) Premise:  All things that do not exist are things such that, even if they did exist, then their non-existence would be possible, i.e., they would be able to not-exist.
(2) Premise:  That-than-which-nothing-greater-can-be-conceived is something such that, if it did exist, then its non-existence would be impossible, i.e., it could not not-exist.
CONCLUSION:    Therefore, that-than-which-nothing-greater-can-be- conceived is NOT something which does not exist.
PART II
(1)Premise:  If that-than-which-nothing-greater- can-be-conceived is NOT something which does not exist, then that-than-which-nothing-greater-can- be-conceived DOES exist.
(2) Premise:   As established in PART I above, that-than-which-nothing-greater-can-be-conceived is NOT something which does not exist.
CONCLUSION:    Therefore, that-than-which-nothing-greater-can-be-conceived DOES exist.
PART III
(1) Premise:  By the word "God" is simply meant *that-than-which-nothing-greater-can-be-conceived.*
(2) Premise:   As established in PART II above, that-than-which-nothing-greater-can-be-conceived DOES exist.
CONCLUSION:  Therefore, God DOES exist.

It should now be apparent that the slighting attitude taken by most philosophers toward the ontological argument is not justified. Anselm's argument cannot with fairness be regarded as merely a quaint piece of sophistry, not to be taken seriously. On the contrary, it is a highly subtle and potentially cogent attempt at proving God's existence. It merits careful and sustained attention.

## The Cosmological Argument

Let us look next at the so-called "cosmological argument" for God's existence. This particular theistic proof is sometimes associated with the name of Thomas Aquinas (A.D. 1224-1274). However, it is an extremely ancient argument, and has had many able proponents during the course of the history of philosophy. The central idea of the cosmological argument, strictly speaking, is that the bare fact of the existence of the universe (i.e., the "cosmos") points unmistakably to the existence of God. However, some particular fact about the universe is often stressed in order to legitimize the logical movement from "The universe exists" to "God exists." Thus, in actual formulations of the cosmological argument, one or another of three notions tends to figure centrally. More specifically, it is customary to state this argument in terms of either the idea of *motion*, that of *causation*, or that of *contingency*. In what follows I shall attempt to state the cosmological argument in terms of the idea of EVENT-DETERMINATION. As far as traditional modes of expression are concerned, the formulation which I shall propose is most similar to that in terms of causation, i.e., to what is called the "first cause" version of the cosmological argument.

For the sake of concision, we may speak simply of DETERMINATION, keeping in mind that, in the present context, this word has reference specifically to EVENTS. That is, by "determining" is meant any instance of making-a-thing-happen.

Before considering the proposed formulation, however, let us be entirely clear concerning the sense in which the word "determination" is to be used. We need at this point to take cognizance of two different types of determining. The one sort of determination may be characterized as *successional*, and the other as *co-existential*. These may be considered in turn.

Taking the verb "to exist" in its broadest sense, which is applicable not only to entities, but also to states-of-affairs and happenings, we may say that "successional determination" refers to all instances of making-a-thing-exist insofar as the thing-made-to-exist is non-existent prior to the act of determining, and *comes into* existence by means of this act of determining. With this type of determination, that-which-is-determined FOLLOWS, i.e., comes into existence AFTER its determinant is already in existence. For example, waves on the surface of a body of water may be said to be determined by the action of wind. Moreover, this is a case of successional determination; for, the waves were at first non-existent, and only afterwards came into existence, through the action of the wind.

On the other hand, co-existential determination is the sort of determination in which the determinant and the thing-that-is-determined always exist together (at the same time), but nonetheless, where the existence of the thing-that-is-determined DEPENDS ON the determinant. That is to say, in co-existential determination the thing-made-to-exist does not come into existence through the action of that-which-causes-it-exist, but rather has always existed *together with* its determinant; or, conversely, it could be said that the determinant did not precede (did not exist at any time without) the thing determined. An example that is sometimes used to illustrate this is that of the sun. We may regard the central body of the sun as the determinant of the light that emanates from it. The light may be viewed as existing by means of the sun, without one's having to suppose either that the sun existed *prior to* the existence of the light, or that the sun brought the light INTO EXISTENCE through its action. Thus, we may consider light's emanating from the sun as illustrating what is meant by "co-existential determination." (What is important here, of course, is not the strict accuracy of the assumptions made concerning the sun, but rather the *use* of such assumptions *to clarify* the notion of co-existential determination.)

Now, some versions of the cosmological argument employ the concept of successional determination, while others invoke that of co-existential determination. For present purposes, however, we can put aside the latter idea. For, the particular formulation which is to be proposed appeals exclusively to the notion of successional determination.

The cosmological argument may now be expressed as follows:

PART I
(1) Premise: If the series of determinants for any given event is infinite, then no event has ever actually happened.
(2) Premise: It is obviously a mistake to say that no event has ever actually happened.
CONCLUSION: Therefore, it is a mistake to say that the series of determinants for any given event is infinite.
PART II
(1) Premise: If it is a mistake to say that the series of determinants for any given event is infinite, then there must exist a determinant that is itself UNDETERMINED.
(2) Premise: As established in PART I above, it is in fact a mistake to say that the series of determinants for any given event

is infinite.

CONCLUSION: Therefore, there must exist a determinant that is itself UNDETERMINED.

PART III

(1) Premise: By the word "God" is simply meant *a determinant that is itself UNDETERMINED*.

(2) Premise: As established in PART II above, there does exist a determinant that is itself UNDETERMINED.

CONCLUSION: Therefore, God does exist.

In order to see any plausibility in this argument, we must focus attention on its key premise, i.e., on premise (1) of PART I. According to this premise, an event that could only be brought about by an INFINITE series of determinants would never actually occur. But what justification is there for making such a claim? In order to support this claim, proponents of the cosmological argument typically invoke the idea that "infinite regression" is impossible. Let us discuss this point in greater detail.

When we speak of an infinite series of determinants, the function of the adjective "infinite" is to underscore that the series mentioned is to be thought of as UNLIMITED. Thus, in an infinite series of determinants, no matter how many determinants we count, there will still be *more* determinants, over and above the ones counted. That is, if a series of determinants is truly infinite, then the process of going through, or counting, these determinants could never come to an end, could never *be finished*.

Now, in general, it is certain that no event can happen until after *all* that is required for its occurrence has been fulfilled. Consequently, if the occurrence of a certain series of determinants is required in order for some particular event to happen, then all of the determinants in the required series must occur successively, *before* the event in question can happen. In other words, all of the determinants in the series would first have to occur, one after another, and then the event would happen.

Let us suppose, now, that some particular event, E, has an infinite series of determinants. In that case, E can only occur after all of the determinants in this infinite series have successively occurred. But, this process in which the determinants of E occur successively could never be completed. Moreover, if this process of fulfilling the requirements for E's occurrence could never be completed, then E itself would never actually happen. This, essentially, is the line of reasoning by means of which most proponents of the cosmological argument would seek to support premise (1) of PART I in the above formulation.

Let us, now, look at premise (1) of PART II. This premise says, in substance, the following: If no event has an infinite series of determinants, then we must infer the existence of an UNDETERMINED determinant, i.e., the existence of something that *makes other things exist*, but which itself *is not made to exist by anything whatsoever*. Again, we may ask: What basis is there for making such a claim?

The cosmological argument assumes that every event that *actually happens* has a FINITE series of determinants. Moreover, that the series of determinants leading up to any given event is finite implies that there is a FIRST determinant in the series. Now, it is evident that both the event in question, and all of the determinants that intervene between this event and the FIRST determinant, are DETERMINED. That is, the event itself, and each of the intervening determinants, is brought-INTO-EXISTENCE, or made-to-OCCUR. However, the FIRST determinant cannot have been brought into existence, or made to occur. For, if it has been brought into existence, then either (a) It was brought into existence *by itself*; or (b) It was brought into existence *by something other than itself*; or (c) It was brought into existence *by nothing*. But, as has been noted by many individuals during the course of the history of philosophy, (a), (b), and (c) are untenable on purely logical grounds.

Thus, it cannot be correct to say that it was brought into existence by itself, because in order for it to bring itself into existence, *it* would have to exist already. In other words, if it brought itself into existence, then, since what is non-existent cannot bring anything into existence, it would have to have already been in existence at the very time when it did not exist. Consequently, from a purely logical standpoint, (a) is untenable.

Moreover, it cannot be true that it was brought into existence by something other than itself. For, in that case, it would not be the FIRST determinant in the series. And surely it cannot be correct to say that the FIRST determinant is not the FIRST determinant. Thus, alternative (b) is equally unacceptable.

As for alternative (c), if we say that it was brought into existence by nothing, then--as many have noted--there are at least two different ways in which this statement could be interpreted. First, this might mean that it was nothing itself that actively caused it to come into existence, i.e., that nothing *actively did* the producing. But, surely this cannot be correct, for nothing, strictly speaking, cannot DO anything, and consequently cannot produce anything. "Nothing" is not anything at all; it is absolute non-existence. And absolute non-existence can neither *be*, nor *do*, nor bring about anything whatsoever. The most that we can say about nothing is simply that *it is nothing*.

But, when we say that it was brought into existence by nothing, we might mean something altogether different. This statement might simply mean that *there is not anything* which brought it into existence. In other words, the statement might be taken to mean that it simply came into existence without having needed anything to bring it into existence. This is clearly something quite different from saying that it was NOTHING that actively did the producing which resulted in its existence. But, if we say that it simply came into existence without having been brought into existence *by anything*, this also is implausible. For, if it initially did not exist--in the sense of being absolutely non-existent--and then subsequently came into existence, then there is no way in which we could interpret this which would not force the conclusion that NOTHING can become something. That is, we would be logically compelled to say that NOTHING actually *became* something. But, nothing can no more BECOME something, than it can *be*, *do*, or *produce* something. Thus, it would appear that alternative (c) must also be rejected. Since, then, alternatives (a), (b), and (c) are all untenable propositions, it must be concluded that a FIRST determinant is necessarily UNDETERMINED.

Let us review the main points. For any *finite* series of determinants, we are logically compelled to admit the existence of a FIRST determinant. Moreover, from what has been said, it follows that a FIRST determinant must itself be undetermined. That is, a FIRST determinant cannot have been brought *into existence*. And this amounts to saying that a FIRST determinant is necessarily an ETERNAL reality, in the sense of having always existed.

In PART III of the cosmological argument, as formulated above, the first premise suggests that the expression "determinant that is itself

UNDETERMINED" constitutes an adequate designation for God. If an analysis of the conceptual content of this expression were actually to lead us to the principal divine attributes, then this suggestion would possess credibility. The 17th century British philosopher, John Locke, having set forth an admirably clear version of the cosmological argument, proceeds through the initial stages of precisely such an analysis. Both his formulation of the argument, and the subsequent analysis are presented in the following quotation from his *Essay*:

...I think I may take for a truth, which every one's certain knowledge assures him of, beyond the liberty of doubting, viz., that he is *something that actually exists.*
In the next place, man knows, by an intuitive certainty, that bare *nothing can no more produce any real being, than it can be equal to two right angles.* If a man knows not that non-entity, or the absence of all being, cannot be equal to two right angles, it is impossible he should know any demonstration of Euclid. If, therefore, we know there is some real being, and that non-entity cannot produce any real being, it is an evident demonstration, that *from eternity there has been something; since* what was not from eternity had a beginning; and what had a beginning must be produced by something else.
Next, it is evident, that what had its being and beginning from another, must also have all that which is in and belongs to its being from another too. All the powers it has must be owing to and received from the same source. This eternal source, then, of all being must also be the source and original of all power; and *so this eternal Being must be also the most powerful.*
Again, a man finds in *himself* perception and knowledge. We have then got one step further; and we are certain now that there is not only some being, but some knowing, intelligent being in the world. There was a time, then, when there was no knowing being, and when knowledge began to be; or else there has been also *a knowing being from eternity.* If it be said, there was a time when no being had any knowledge, when that eternal being was void of all understanding; I reply, that then it was impossible there should ever have been any knowledge: it being as impossible that things wholly void of knowledge, and operating blindly, and without any perception, should produce a knowing being, as it is impossible that a triangle should make itself three angles bigger than two right

ones. For it is as repugnant to the idea of senseless matter, that it should put into itself sense, perception, and knowledge, as it is repugnant to the idea of a triangle, that it should put into itself greater angles than two right ones.

Thus, from the consideration of ourselves, and what we infallibly find in our own constitutions, our reason leads us to the knowledge of this certain and evident truth, *That there is an eternal, most powerful, and most knowing Being*; which whether any one will please to call God, it matters not. The thing is evident; and from this idea duly considered, will easily be deduced all those other attributes, which we ought to ascribe to this eternal Being.[7]

Thus, we see that Locke undertook to ferret out the various divine attributes, on the basis of what he had established in the initial phase of his argumentation. In doing this, he seems to have anticipated, and sought to remove beforehand, one of the most common objections against the cosmological argument. That objection is as follows: Even if the cosmological argument is sound, it only succeeds in establishing the existence of a determinant that is itself UNDETERMINED; it does not show that this UNDETERMINED determinant has the various attributes traditionally ascribed to God, e.g., intelligence, mercy, wisdom, justice, kindness, and so forth. In other words, what if this UNDETERMINED determinant is merely a "blind," and morally indifferent ground-of-existence, or source-of-all-being? In that case, the objection states, proving the existence of this UNDETERMINED determinant does not really amount to proving that *God* exists. But, the approach taken by Locke in the above-cited passage represents one obvious way in which proponents of the cosmological argument may respond to this criticism.

### The Teleological Argument

The third theistic proof which we shall consider in this chapter is commonly referred to as the "teleological argument" for God's existence. Since the key concept utilized in this argument is that of "design," it is also sometimes given the name "argument from design." And, to begin with, it is just this concept concerning which we need to get a clear understanding.

In discussions of the teleological argument, attempts at clarifying the concept of design often make use of the example of "Paley's watch."

William Paley, an 18th century theologian and author of a work entitled *Natural Theology*, seeks to elucidate the idea of design by means of the following, imaginary situation. Imagine that a certain individual is walking through a desert island. As this hypothetical individual proceeds through the desert, he comes across a series of objects. The first object which he comes across is, let us say, a rock. He now raises the question: How did this rock come into existence? Moreover, in reflecting on this, he comes to the conclusion that the existence of the rock can satisfactorily be explained in terms of the operation of wholly blind, mechanical force. But, as he continues to walk through the desert, he comes across another object, namely a watch. Here, he poses the same question to himself that he raised earlier regarding the rock. He finds in the case of the watch, however, that he is NOT able to ascribe its existence to the operation of *blind, mechanical* force. Rather, in examining the watch, he discovers that it possesses characteristics which compel him to believe that it can only have come into existence as a result of *intelligent* action. In other words, he observes that the characteristics of the watch are such as to point unmistakably to the existence of a watch-maker.

Now, those characteristics of the watch which suggest an intelligent origin exemplify what is meant by "design." In the context of discussions of the teleological argument, "design" refers to precisely that which the watch possesses and the rock lacks. By "design" is meant that the presence of which in the watch points to intelligent action, and the absence of which from the rock suggests purely mechanical action. More explicitly stated, to be characterized by design consists in the fact of being constituted in such a way as to be either intrinsically of value, or conducive to valued outcomes, and this to such an extent as cannot be regarded as fortuitous.

The central thesis of the teleological argument is that the universe is characterized by design in exactly the sense indicated above. That is, if we consider attentively the universe and its component parts, then, supposedly, we will discover that they possess characteristics which compel us to conclude that their existence can only be explained in terms of intelligent action. Just as the watch points to the existence of a watch-maker, the universe itself is thought to point to the existence of a universe-maker. The teleological argument can be expressed as follows:

PART I

(1) Premise: If the universe exhibits design, then there must exist a supremely intelligent reality that has given the universe the design it exhibits.

(2) Premise: In fact, the universe does exhibit design.

CONCLUSION:       Therefore, there does exist a supremely intelligent reality that has given the universe the design it exhibits.

PART II

(1) Premise:   By the word "God" is simply meant a *supremely intelligent reality that has given the universe the design it exhibits.*

(2) Premise:   As established in PART I above, there does exist a supremely intelligent reality that has given the universe the design it exhibits.

CONCLUSION:  Therefore, God does exist.

Now, in seeking to support the claim that the universe exhibits design, most proponents of the teleological argument call attention to various facts concerning the construction of living things, and/or the arrangement and functioning of the component parts of living things. William Paley, for instance, in his exposition of the teleological argument, gives prolonged consideration to the functioning and mode of construction of the human eye. Paley's point, of course, is that if we sufficiently familiarize ourselves with the characteristics of the human eye, then, ineluctably, we will be led to infer that a designer-of-the-eye exists.

A host of other, similar observations could be made with regard to living things. If, for example, we consider the human skeletal system, we will observe the manner in which the various bones fit together neatly at the joints, and in precisely such a way as to facilitate useful movements. We will observe, moreover, how the various muscles are attached to the bones *in just the right places*--again, ostensibly so as to allow for the particular movements that are requisite in performing the tasks of life. Thus, it can be seen how the bones and muscles of the body inter-relate harmoniously, and co-operate for the attainment of desirable ends. Another example that is frequently cited is that of the wings of birds, which seem to have been skillfully adapted for the purpose of flight.

Outside of the sphere of the living, attention could be directed to such things as the orderly arrangement of the parts of our solar system, the rotation of the earth on its axis (with the consequent alternation of day and night), and the movement of the earth around the sun (with the concomitant cycle of the seasons). The regular alternation of day and night, and the constant return of fall, winter, spring, and summer seem clearly to relate in a harmonious way to various facets of human life and activity (e.g., to waking, sleeping, planting, growing, reaping, and so on). And proponents of the teleological arguments are likely to maintain that such felicitous arrangements are indicative of intelligent planning.

In discussions of the teleological argument, it is customary to call attention to certain criticisms based on the work of the empiricist philosopher, David Hume (A.D. 1711-1776), and the evolutionary theorist, Charles Darwin (A.D. 1809-1882). But the central point of such criticisms is simply this: To assume the existence of an intelligent maker is not the ONLY way to explain those features of the universe that seem to constitute design. That is to say, the basic objection is that there are OTHER ways of accounting for apparent design. Thus, for instance, random mutations and natural selection--taken together--might be proposed as an alternative way of explaining what is ostensibly design in the bodies of living things.

However, what needs to be kept in mind concerning such criticisms is that they cannot justly be regarded as capable of actually refuting the teleological argument. If the ALTERNATIVE explanation offered were shown ultimately to be the ONLY POSSIBLE explanation, then it would cease to be merely an *alternative*, and the teleological argument would stand refuted. But insofar as any given criticism of the teleological argument is based on what in fact is merely an alternative explanation of ostensible design, the proponent of the teleological argument, at most, is only forced to re-formulate his argument in inductive form, and then view it as weakened in some degree, due to the possibility of an alternative explanation.

But some who find the teleological argument plausible would entirely reject all explanations other than that of an intelligent designer. This is the position taken in the following passage, as part of a more general indictment of the materialistic mode of thinking. It is a quotation from the writings of the Afro-American theologian and social activist, Martin Luther King, Jr.:

This man-centered foolishness has had a long and ofttimes disas-
trous reign in the history of mankind. Sometimes it is theoretically
expressed in the doctrine of materialism, which contends that reality may be explained in terms of matter in motion, that life is "a
physiological process with physiological meaning," that man is a
transient accident of protons and electrons travelling blind, that
thought is a temporary product of grey matter, and that the events
of history are an interaction of matter and motion operating by the
principle of necessity. Having no place for God or for eternal
ideas, materialism is opposed to both theism and idealism.
The materialistic philosophy leads inevitably into a dead-end street
in an intellectually senseless world. To believe that human personality is the result of the fortuitous interplay of atoms and electrons
is as absurd as to believe *that a monkey by hitting typewriter keys
at random will eventually produce a Shakespearean play.* Sheer
magic! It is much more sensible to say with Sir James Jeans, the
physicist, that "the universe seems to be nearer to a great thought
than to a great machine," or with Arthur Balfour, the philosopher,
that "we know too much about matter to be materialists."
Materialism is a weak flame that is blown out by the breath of
mature thinking.[8]

### The Moral Argument

We shall consider a fourth argument in favor of God's existence. It
is usually called the "moral argument." Dr. Felix Adler (1851-1933), a
past president of the American Philosophical Association and founder of
the Ethical Culture movement, presents a form of the moral argument in
the following passage from his book *The Religion of Duty*:

Can there be a rigorous obligation--and the moral obligation is
such--to achieve that which is unattainable? Can the demand for a
justice, higher than has ever yet been seen, be a deception? On
the other hand, if the demand for justice is realizable, then, in the
nature of things, there must be provision that it shall be realized;
then there must be, as it has been expressed, "a Power that makes
for righteousness."
So, I believe that there is a higher Being, an ultimate, divine
Reality in things. This Being is not like a man, is not He, or She
or It, did not make the world, as a carpenter makes a table, or as

an architect builds a house. In the attempt to describe this Being, language faints, imagination grows dizzy, thought is paralyzed. On moral grounds, and in the last analysis on moral grounds only, I assume the existence of such a Being. All that I can say, by way of description, is that there really exists that which corresponds to the moral ideal, that there is a Power back of the effort toward righteousness, which gives effect to it, beyond our finite power.[9]

The following is a simplified reconstruction of the moral argument, as it is expressed by Adler in the above quotation:

(1) Premise: If God does not exist, then there is no such thing as morality.
(2) Premise: But, it is a mistake to say that there is no such thing as morality.
CONCLUSION: Therefore, God does exist.

In order to gain a better understanding of this argument, let us focus attention on the word "morality." What is the meaning of this term? In the ensuing lines, I shall give a brief outline of one possible answer to this question, in order to see to what extent the moral argument can be viewed as plausible in light of the answer proposed. And in undertaking to do this, the first thing to note is that the term "morality" is ambiguous. It may be used in at least three distinct, albeit closely related, senses. In one sense of the word, we may say that morality is a predicate of *actions*; in another sense, that it is a predicate of *dispositions*; and in a third sense, that it is a predicate of *persons*. Accordingly, we may speak of moral actions, of moral dispositions, and of moral persons; hence, the exact definition of "moral" would have to be different in each case, due to the differing applications.

However, these different senses of the word "morality" are interconnected in a way such that to adopt a particular conception of any one of them would pretty much dictate how the other two would have to be defined. Consequently, in attempting to arrive at an answer to the question raised above, it will suffice to focus initially on just one of these applications of the word; and, afterwards, we can determine what consequences this has for the remaining two. Thus, to begin with, we can look at moral *action*. What exactly is meant by "moral action"?

It seems clear that an adequate account of the nature of human action cannot restrict itself merely to outward behavior. Rather, human action most assuredly has an interior, mental dimension; and the significance of this interior dimension of action is such that no outward performance emanating from a human being can ever be fully understood, or accurately assessed, without reference to it. Let us conceive of human action, then, as characterized by a three-dimensional structure. More specifically, let us think of an action as possessed of a *cognitive* dimension, an *emotive* dimension, and a *behavioral* dimension. By "cognitive dimension" is meant that aspect of action which consists in *thinking* or knowing; by "emotive dimension" is meant that component of action which consists in *feeling* or *affect*; and by "behavioral dimension" is meant the facet of action that consists in *outward* performances or doings.

Now, when an action is described as "moral," this description has applicability at all three levels mentioned. Moreover, for the sake of the present discussion, let us make the following supposition: To say that a particular action is moral amounts to saying that that action constitutes a *correct* ascription of worth, i.e., an ascription of worth to that which *actually does possess worth.* Consistently with this, we can say that a moral action, in its cognitive dimension, is an acknowledgement of worth at the level of THOUGHT; that a moral action, in its emotive dimension, is an acknowledgement of worth at the level of FEELING; and that a moral action, in its behavioral dimension, is an acknowledgement of worth at the level of OUTWARD PERFORMANCES. In other words, we may conceive of moral action as consisting in the correct ascription of worth by means of our faculties of thinking, feeling, and outward-doing.

Now, if to act morally is to attribute worth to that which actually possesses worth, then moral dispositions are simply the corresponding "springs" of action. Moral dispositions are the dispositions which underlie moral action, and which--taken together--constitute what is called "character." Furthermore, if moral action consists in correct ascriptions of worth, and if moral dispositions are the dispositions which underlie such action, then we may say that a moral person is simply a person who possesses such moral dispositions, i.e., who is "disposed" to act morally. Thus, a moral person, a person who possesses "character," is one who is disposed to ascribe worth--by means of the faculties of thinking, feeling, and outward doing--to that which actually does possess worth.

From what has been said, it would follow that the common thread running through all three varieties of moral discourse (i.e., talk concerning moral actions, moral dispositions, and moral persons) is the idea of correct-ascriptions-of-worth. Let us re-formulate the moral argument in such a way as to make explicit use of this idea.

(1) Premise: If God does not exist, then there is no such thing as a correct ascription of worth.
(2) Premise: But surely there is such a thing as a correct ascription of worth.
CONCLUSION: Consequently, God does exist.

According to premise (1) of this re-formulation, in order for there to be any such thing as a correct ascription of worth, God must exist. How can this claim be supported? In the above quotation, Dr. Adler makes reference to something "in the nature of things" that provides for "the demand for justice"; he also talks about "a Power that makes for righteousness." The terms "justice" and "righteousness" are synonyms for "morality," and both of these synonyms have a pattern of ambiguity similar to that of the word "morality." We may say, then, that when Adler refers to a something that-provides-for-the demand-for-JUSTICE, and to a Power-that-makes-for-RIGHTEOUSNESS, what he speaks of could equally well be described as a something-in-the-nature-of-things-that-provides-for-the-demand-for-MORALITY, and as a Power-that-makes-for- MORALITY. Moreover, in each pair, the two designations may be regarded as equivalent in meaning. Hence, for the sake of brevity, let us restrict ourselves to the use of just one of these designations, namely, "a Power that makes for MORALITY."

Now, in order to see how premise (1) might be supported, it needs to be noted that in speaking of a Power-that-makes-for-MORALITY, Adler is referring to God. What is the significance of saying that God is that which makes for morality? In the light of our previous account of morality in terms of correct worth-ascriptions, we may say that such a claim concerning God amounts to saying that God is *that which makes for correct worth-ascriptions*. But what exactly is it that makes for correct worth-ascriptions? What is it, in other words, that makes it possible for there to be such a thing as a correct ascription-of-worth? One obvious answer to this is that worth can be correctly ascribed to things, only on condition that THINGS ACTUALLY POSSESS

WORTH. Thus, for instance, it might be said that the *inner potencies* (i.e., the concealed root-dispositions) which underlie intelligence, kindness, fairness, generosity, love, etc., are what constitutes WORTH in persons. And, in that case worth can be correctly ascribed to persons, only on condition that persons actually possess such inner potencies or basic dispositions. But, things actually possess worth, only on condition that THERE IS SUCH A THING as worth, i.e., inherent excellence or goodness. Ultimately, then, that which makes for correct worth-ascriptions is a worth, or fundamental goodness, actually residing in things objectively, to which our interior judgments may conform or correspond.

Accordingly, if by the word "God" we mean this very worth, this fundamental goodness itself, then it is clear that if God does not exist, then there can be no such thing as a correct ascription of worth. That is, if God is this very worth, this fundamental goodness itself, then premise (1) in our re-formulation is true. Moreover, Adler at least, as one proponent of the moral argument, would be likely to invoke such a conception of God, in seeking to support this premise.

As for premise (2), the typical advocate of the moral argument appeals to some such notion as that of a "sense of duty" or "feeling of obligation." The gist of this appeal is the claim that we have a *sense* or *feeling* that certain worth-ascriptions are correct, and that this very sense or feeling somehow justifies us in regarding the mentioned worth-ascriptions as in fact correct. But, this approach seems altogether lacking in persuasive force. Consequently, since its soundness depends on the truth of both of its premises, it is not at all clear that the moral argument itself has succeeded in its aim.

However, there is another more charitable way of looking at the moral argument. Specifically, it is possible to regard this argument as having as its conclusion not the statement "God exists," but rather the statement "The belief in morality can be held with logical consistency only if it is conjoined with a belief in the existence of God." This essentially is the approach taken by the German philosopher Immanuel Kant (A.D. 1724-1804). Understood in keeping with this, the basic line of reasoning could be loosely stated as follows: "God" signifies that *objective standard* a reference to which is needed, in order for actions, dispositions, and persons to be classified as moral. Hence, the goal of becoming a moral person would be attainable only if God existed. Whoever, therefore, believes in, and has resolved to work toward, the goal of becoming a *moral* person, must proceed on the assumption that God exists; for, otherwise, the pursuit of this goal would not be a reasonable one.

## The Mystic's Argument

Let us briefly discuss one further argument in support of God's existence. This argument appeals to the notion of "direct experience." Among philosophers and theologians, the view that God can be directly experienced is often referred to as "mysticism." The term "mysticism" is etymologically related to the word "mystery." Both of these words come from the Greek word "mystos," which in turn is derived from the Greek verb "myein." The verb "myein" means *to be closed*, where this is said specifically of the eyes and lips. These etymological points bring out the main idea of mysticism. For, the world is HIDDEN from the person whose eyes are closed, and one whose lips are closed does NOT UTTER any statements concerning the world. Consistently with its etymology, then, the word "mysticism" suggests a certain kind of CONCEALMENT, and a consequent SILENCE. Briefly, mysticism is the belief that GOD is *concealed* within us, and that we are *silent* regarding God in consequence of this concealment. Mysticism is sometimes described as the "perennial philosophy," and as the common factor in the various religions of the world. (Some of its basic assumptions were alluded to previously in our discussion of points of agreement between the different religions.) It can be defined more explicitly in terms of the following five theses:

(1) God, i.e., Divinity, resides somehow within us, and within all things.
(2) In the ordinary state of consciousness which prevails among human beings, God, this Divinity within us, is HIDDEN from our view, by a "covering," so to speak.
(3) This "covering" that keeps God hidden from view is misguided attachment.
(4) Misguided attachment can gradually be removed, through persistence in the performance of certain spiritual exercises (for example, meditation, contemplative prayer, intensive cultivation of morality, etc.).
(5) As a result of the removal of this "covering" of misguided at-

tachment, we will come to have a direct experience of God.

Consider, for instance, how these core assumptions of mysticism are expressed in the following statements of Sri Ramakrishna, a recent figure in the Hindu tradition:

> He who does not find God within himself will never find Him outside himself. But he who sees Him in the temple of his soul, sees Him also in the temple of the universe. God is seen when the mind is tranquil. When the sea of the mind is agitated by the wind of desires, it cannot reflect God, and then God-vision is impossible.[10]

Now, since the argument which we are going to consider at this point is based on mysticism, it can be referred to simply as the "mystic's argument." In this context, the word "mystic" means *a person who either has had a direct experience of God, or at least believes that such an experience is possible.* Before presenting a reconstruction of the mystic's argument, let us look at another short passage from the *Teachings of Sri Ramakrishna.* This passage gives an account of Sri Ramakrishna's reply, on a certain occasion, to being questioned concerning the existence of God.

> "Do you believe in God, sir?"
> "Yes," the Master replied.
> "Can you prove it, sir?"
> "Yes."
> "How?"
> "Because I see Him just as I see you here, only very much more intensely."[11]

The response which Sri Ramakrishna gives to his questioner here amounts to a succinct statement of what we have designated "the mystic's argument." The following is a slightly more explicit formulation of this argument:

> (1) Premise: Whatever can actually be experienced directly does exist.
> (2) Premise: God can actually be experienced directly.
> CONCLUSION: Therefore, God does exist.

Premise (1) of this argument would appear to be entirely uncontroversial. For, from the fact that something is directly experienced, it would seem to follow inescapably that this something has some type of status as an existing thing. There is a difficulty with premise (2), however. For as regards the direct experience of God, there are two possibilities: Either (a) one has had this direct experience, or (b) one has not had this direct experience. Now, suppose that one has had this direct experience; in that case one is in a position to confirm premise (2). But, at the same time, if one has actually had this experience, then--even though one is in a position to confirm premise (2)--One no longer needs premise (2); for, the argument of which this premise is a part is no longer required for the purpose of proving that God exists. The point here is that adducing an *argument* is necessary, or useful, only in connection with that which is NOT directly experienced, and whose existence, consequently, must be rationally INFERRED. Thus, for example, if one has actually seen the sun, then one is not in need of an argument to prove that the sun exists. Once we have seen the sun itself, its existence has become a matter of direct experience, and no longer needs to be rationally *inferred.*

On the other hand, there is alternative (b), namely the possibility that one has *not* had this direct experience of God. If one has not had this direct experience of God, then one is not in a position to confirm premise (2). But, it is precisely in the absence of such direct experience that one has need of the argument in which premise (2) occurs.

Thus, it may be said with respect to the mystic's argument that insofar as we are in a position to verify that it is a sound argument, we have no need of it; and, as long as we stand in need of this argument, we will never be in a position to verify that it is sound. But, if--at the very time when one has need of this argument--one cannot confirm it, and if one no longer needs it once one has become able to confirm it, then there is no possibility that the mystic's argument can be of any real service to the theist who wants to be rationally persuaded that God exists. This applies to the mystic's argument in the form in which it is stated above.

Nevertheless, accumulated historical testimony as to mystical experience, as well as contemporary reports of direct experiences of God, CAN be invoked in the construction of a pertinent argument. Rather than actually asserting that God exists, the conclusion of this alternative form of the mystic's argument would amount to a recommendation; it would constitute a prescription for all those who desire to be convinced of God's existence by, so to speak, seeing God with their own "eyes." The argument which I have in mind is the following:

(1) Premise:   If large numbers of individuals throughout history have repeatedly claimed that they arrived at a DIRECT EXPERIENCE of God, as a result of following a certain path (i.e., as a result of persevering in certain spiritual exercises) then whoever desires to be convinced of God's existence by DIRECT EXPERIENCE should undertake to follow the indicated path (i.e., should undertake to perform the indicated spiritual exercises in order to determine whether or not such an experience will actually come about).

(2) Premise:   Throughout history large numbers of individuals have, in fact, repeatedly claimed that they arrived at a DIRECT EXPERIENCE of God, as a result of following a certain path (i.e., as a result of persevering in certain spiritual exercises).

CONCLUSION:   Therefore, whoever desires to be convinced of God's existence by DIRECT EXPERIENCE should undertake to follow the indicated path (i.e., should undertake to perform the indicated spiritual exercises in order to determine whether or not such an experience will actually come about).

Premise (1) of this argument is a "conditional," i.e., an if-then statement. It is not likely to evoke any serious opposition. The truth of this premise would appear to be obvious. For, anyone who wishes to achieve a certain result would be well-advised to follow the example of others who claim--by some particular means--to have achieved that result. This point can be made in a more concrete fashion, through the use of a comparison.

Imagine that there is an extremely tall building located in a rustic setting, say, at the center of a small town. Imagine, moreover, that there are several ladders firmly attached to the facade of this building, and that these ladders extend all the way to the top. Now, let us suppose that, despite the visual prominence of this edifice, the majority of the townspeople do not pay very much attention to it. Nevertheless, during the course of the town's history an appreciable number of the town's inhabitants have approached the facade, stepped onto a ladder, and undertaken the long and arduous climb to the roof. Let us assume that all of these individuals, upon returning from their visit to the roof, give to the other townspeople a basically similar report as to what they saw. Specifically, on their return, all of these individuals have invariably stated that there is a vast treasure spread out over the roof, an abundance of gold, silver, jewels, and precious stones of every sort. But, although this treasure is said to be a spectacle of utmost beauty and ineffable splendor, it was never possible for anyone to bring back a tangible item attesting to its existence. The visitors-to-the-roof, on their return, were only able to give verbal testimony as to the existence of this treasure, and to CALL ATTENTION TO THE SEVERAL LADDERS on the facade, which led up to the roof. Suppose, now, that some particular townsperson expresses a desire to see this treasure for himself/herself. Surely it would be appropriate for this townsperson to utter the following conditional statement: If large numbers of individuals, during the course of our town's history, have repeatedly claimed that they arrived at a direct experience of a "treasure," as a result of climbing a ladder at the facade, then whoever desires to be convinced of the existence of this treasure, by direct experience, should undertake to climb one of the ladders. The alternative form of the mystic's argument which we are now considering presupposes that the case is altogether similar in connection with one who desires to "see" God for himself/herself. That is, it would be entirely appropriate for such a person to utter the conditional statement which occurs as premise (1) of the above argument.

As for premise (2), a survey of philosophico-religious history shows that an impressive number of individuals, from the most ancient times down to the present, have given surprisingly similar accounts of an alleged direct experience of God. These accounts of mystical experience have emanated from individuals widely separated, not only in time, but also geographically and culturally. The initiates of the ancient Egyptian mysteries, the rishis (i.e., "seers") of ancient India, the Neoplatonist thinker Plotinus, the Islamic mystic Ibn al-Arabi, Thomas Aquinas, Meister Eckhart, St. John of the Cross, St. Teresa of Avila, Emanuel Swedenborg, William Blake, Abdu 'l-Baha, Sri Ramakrishna, Rudolf Steiner, Sri Aurobindo, and Martin Luther King, Jr. are just a small fraction of the total number of individuals who, during the course of history, have spoken of a direct experience of God. Accordingly, premise (2) can easily be verified. Thus, since both of its premises appear to be plausible, and since its form is clearly valid in form, we are justified in concluding that the mystic's argument is sound. That is, the alternative form of the argument stated above does succeed in establishing its conclusion.

*Notes*

[1]St. Anselm, *Basic Writings* (La Salle, IL: Open Court Publishing, 1962), p. 54.
[2]St. Anselm, Ibid., (La Salle, IL: Open Court Publishing, 1962), p. 309. (Gaunilon's reply is reproduced in the appendix of this book.)_
[3]Ibid., p. 327. (Emphasis added.)
[4]Ibid., pp. 54-55.
[5]Ibid., p. 56.
[6]Ibid., p. 320.
[7]Beck, Lewis White (ed.), *18-Century Philosophy* (New York: The Free Press, 1966), pp. 51-52.
[8]King, Martin Luther, *Strength to Love* (Philadelphia: Fortress Press, 1963), p. 71. (Emphasis added.)
[9]Adler, Felix, *The Religion of Duty* (New York: McClure, Phillips & Co., 1905), pp. 37 and 39.
[10]Budhananda, Swami (ed.), *Teachings of Sri Ramakrishna* (Calcutta: Advaita Ashrama, 1975), p. 269.
[11]Ibid., p. 276.

CHAPTER FIVE:


THE CONCEPT OF LIFE
AFTER DEATH

CHAPTER FIVE:  The Concept of Life After Death

The aim of this chapter is to promote clear thinking about life after death.  More specifically, I shall undertake to carry out several interrelated tasks.  First, the question "What is Spirit?" will be addressed.  For, the notion of spiritual beings is intimately tied to the concept of an afterlife.  The goal here is simply to get clear concerning the CONCEPT of Spirit, not--initially-to prove that such things as spirits actually exist.  (When speaking generally, of spirituality or spirithood, I will use the word "Spirit," with an uppercase "s."  When speaking of individual beings, I will use the expressions "spirit" and "spiritual being," with a lowercase "s.")  Moreover, having gotten clear concerning the basic idea of Spirit, we shall proceed briefly to take note of some of the implications of this idea.  Next, an attempt will be made to clarify what it is we are asking when we raise the question "Is there life after death?"  And finally, some of the major forms which the belief in a life after death can take will be enumerated and briefly discussed.

What is Spirit?

In attempting to achieve clear thoughts about the spiritual, let us begin with the following affirmation:  A spirit is an ENTITY that is characterized by CONSCIOUSNESS and NON-MATERIALITY. If we unpack the inner content of this affirmation, we shall arrive at a clear conception of the nature of a spiritual being. Let us consider in turn the key portions of this affirmation.

What is the significance of saying that a spirit is an entity? By the word "entity," in this context, is meant an *independently existing thing*. But, what is it for a thing to exist independently? To speak of a thing as existing independently is to underscore that it exists in its own right, as something self-contained or complete in itself. To express this more clearly, if we say that a thing exists independently, we mean to stress that the thing in question is not merely a PROPERTY or STATE of something, but rather HAS properties and GOES THROUGH successive states. Alternatively, we may say that an entity is not a property possessED by something, but rather is itself something possessING properties; and similarly, an entity is not a state enterED-and-passED-through by something, but rather is itself something enterING-and-passING-through successive states.

To illustrate, imagine that a soft piece of clay has been successively molded into different shapes. Let us say that we first impose upon the clay a cubical shape, then a pyramidal shape, and finally a spherical shape. What is usually assumed about such a case is that the clay HAS certain properties, and successively GOES THROUGH certain states. The color and size of the clay, for example, would usually be thought of as properties possessed by the clay. And it is commonly supposed that the indicated shapes are merely passing states of the clay, just conditions-of-itself which the clay goes through. Accordingly, we may say that to describe something as an entity, in the present context, is to emphasize that it possesses the kind of status that is commonly ascribed to this clay itself, and that it is not like the color, size, and successive shapes of this clay, which BELONG TO the clay and DEPEND ON it for their existence.

Among philosophers, the traditional term for what we have just attempted to clarify is "substance." To say that something is an entity amounts to saying that it is a substance, in the philosophical sense of the word "substance." However, the disadvantage of using the word "substance" is that, in common parlance, it is employed somewhat differently from how it is employed in philosophy. To the non-philosopher, the word "substance" tends to suggest the idea of a continuous (i.e., endlessly divisible) MATERIAL stuff. But, the philosophic concept of substance is neutral as regards the idea of materiality. In the philosophic sense of the word, a substance is an underlying property-POSSESSOR, irrespective of what particular properties are conceived of as possessed. That is, the properties possessed do not necessarily have to be visualizable, material properties. The concept of substance, purely as such, has no corresponding VISUALIZATION; it can only be apprehended by means of THOUGHT, not through concrete IMAGINATION. Thus, we may use the terms "entity" and "substance" interchangeably; however, if we do so, an effort must be made to keep in mind the indicated neutrality of the word "substance."

Let us return to the questions we raised earlier, namely "What is the significance of saying that a spirit is an entity?" To say that a spirit is an entity amounts to saying that when we conceive of a spirit, we conceive of something which is not merely a property or state BELONGING TO something, but rather something which itself actually POSSESSES properties, and successively PASSES THROUGH different states.

Next, let us consider consciousness. What is the significance of the claim that a spirit is an entity that is characterized by CONSCIOUSNESS? The word "consciousness" is used here, in a very broad sense, to cover all varieties of awareness. To say that a spirit is a CONSCIOUS entity is to say that it is essentially in possession of all varieties of awareness. More explicitly, we may say that, as a *conscious* entity, a spirit must be thought of as sentient, imaginative, attentive, cogitative, affective, volitive, and so on.

To say that a spirit is SENTIENT amounts to saying that it experiences all varieties of sensations. As a sentient entity, a spirit has VISUAL sensations, or SEES; has AUDITORY sensations, or HEARS; has TACTILE sensations, or FEELS; has GUSTATORY sensations, or TASTES; and has OLFACTORY sensations, or SMELLS. Moreover, in the present context, all of the above-mentioned modes of awareness must be thought of exclusively in terms of the INNER EXPERIENCE involved, so that no thought of BODILY sense-organs arises. Thus, with vision, we must think about the actual experience of color and form, without allowing the thought of physical eyes to enter into our conception. Similarly, in the case of hearing, we must think of sound-experience *purely as such*, and not allow the thought of physical ears to intrude. Precisely the same considerations apply in connection with the other varieties of experience enumerated. Briefly, we must think of all of these varieties of awareness as having the same status as the one we commonly ascribe to the inner experiences which arise during a dream.

Now, insofar as various experiences are imposed upon it by outside forces, a spirit is said to be *sentient*. But, a spirit is also an IMAGINA-TIVE entity; for, REPRODUCTIONS of the afore-mentioned experiences can arise from within its own nature. To say that a spirit is IMAGINATIVE amounts to saying that Spirit itself can actually make all varieties of internal mental imagery. As an imaginative entity, a spirit has VISUAL imagery, or inwardly experiences COLOR and FORM; has AUDITORY imagery, or inwardly experiences SOUNDS of all types; has TACTILE imagery, or inwardly experiences reproductions of touch-sensations; has GUSTATORY imagery, or inwardly experiences reproductions of taste-sensations; and has OLFACTORY imagery, or inwardly experiences reproductions of smell-sensations.

To say that a spirit is ATTENTIVE amounts to saying that it performs acts-of-noticing, and acts-of-sustained-examining, that are directed toward its own states of sensing, imagining, and so forth. For example, a spirit may notice the successive states of color-experience and of sound-experience which it passes through during the course of a dream; or a spirit may carefully note the number of distinct items contained within its "visual field" on a particular occasion during waking life.

To say that a spirit is COGITATIVE amounts to saying that it THINKS ABOUT its various states of sensing, imagining, attending, and so on. By means of thinking, a spirit takes awareness of all facets of its interior condition; and it becomes acquainted not only with the passing states of consciousness which it goes through, but also with its own existence as a permanent, or stable, CENTER-of-consciousness.

To say that a spirit is AFFECTIVE amounts to saying that it experiences all varieties of emotion. A spirit loves, hates, fears, rejoices, grieves, and so on.

To say that a spirit is VOLITIVE amounts to saying that it wills, wishes, and chooses.

In short, as previously stated, to say that a spirit is a conscious entity is simply to say that it manifests or displays all possible varieties of awareness.

But let us look a bit more deeply into the claim that a spirit is a conscious entity. In the context of the present discussion, consciousness is assumed to possess two distinguishable aspects. In order to clarify this point, let us make use of the terms "expression" and "potency." By "expression" may be understood *the actual OCCURRENCE of mental states, which reveals underlying power*; and by "potency" may be understood *the underlying mental POWER which is revealed through the actual occurrence of mental states.* Accordingly, as stated previously, consciousness is assumed here to possess two distinguishable facets, namely EXPRESSION and POTENCY. Expression is, so to speak, supra-consciousness, because it stands "above" and is supported by potency; whereas, potency is, so to speak, sub-consciousness, because it stands "beneath" and supports expression.

In its dimension of expression, consciousness consists in the actual occurrence of various mental states; but, in its dimension of potency, it consists in the underlying power, or force, which is manifested when mental states actually occur. Giving some thought to the etymology of each term will assist us to gain greater clarity with respect to these two facets of consciousness. The English word "expression" is derived from the Latin words "ex" and "premere," which mean *out* and *to press*, respectively. And our English word "potency" is derived from the Latin "potere," which means *to be able.*

Now, to say that a spirit is characterized by consciousness implies that we may say such things as these: "A spirit SEES," "A spirit HEARS," "A spirit ATTENDS," "A spirit THINKS," and so forth. But, every such statement logically entails a claim concerning the POTENCY of a spirit. Thus, the statement "A spirit SEES" implies the statement "A spirit CAN see"; "A spirit HEARS" implies "A spirit CAN hear"; and "A spirit THINKS" implies "A spirit CAN think." Therefore, to say that a spirit is characterized by consciousness is not only to point to the fact of EXPRESSION--to the actual occurrence of mental states, or the successive conditions-of-itself-which a spirit passes through. Rather, to say that a spirit is characterized by consciousness is also to point to the fact of POTENCY. And the potency of a spirit is simply the fact that *a spirit* CAN. Let us take note of two further points regarding potency.

Firstly, it needs to be clearly understood that the potency of a spirit--unlike spiritual expression--would have to be unlimited. For, we may say that a spirit, as a conscious entity, CAN engage in infinitely many mental performances, that it has infinitely many specific powers. If we take the word "ability" in it widest sense, so that it covers both active and passive doings, then we may say that a spirit must be conceived of as possessing infinitely many specific abilities. Thus, the *general* potency of a spirit would have to be understood in terms of this multitude of *specific* abilities. From a consideration of just the one example of arithmetical truths, this conclusion would appear to be certain. For insofar as a spirit is conceived of as a conscious entity, it must be understood as being ABLE to contemplate arithmetical truths. And it is certain that both numbers and numerical relationships are infinite, i.e., unending. Moreover, just as a spirit must be conceived of as able to perform the particular mental act of contemplating "5 x 5 = 25," it must also be conceived of as able to contemplate all other arithmetic truths. Consequently, it must be conceived of as able to perform infinitely many mental acts, for, as intimated above, there are infinitely many arithmetic truths.

The second point that I wish to make concerning spiritual potency is that this must be conceived of as a stable or enduring feature of spiritual beings. That is, the potency of a spirit is not a mere possibility. For, the word "possibility" tends to suggest the idea of something that DOES NOT actually exist, but, nonetheless, CAN come to exist. The potency of a spirit is not a mere possibility, in this sense of the word. Moreover, if we understand the etymologically cognate term "potentiality" as a synonym for "possibility," then the potency of a spirit is not a mere potentiality. On the contrary, we must conceive of the potency of a spirit as a *perpetually-existing* characteristic of that spirit. For, spiritual potency must already be in existence PRIOR TO the occurrence of any particular mental state which--on the level of expression--manifests this potency. Thus, a spirit will never actually perform a mental act, unless it is already true, BEFORE the performance of that act, that the spirit CAN perform that act. But, a spirit, by definition, is an entity that performs mental acts. Hence, insofar as spiritual potency has this kind of priority, it must ultimately be said that such potency is a stable or enduring quality of spiritual beings.

Let us now return to the affirmation which we have begun to explicate. The affirmation concerning spirit with which we commenced is this: A spirit is an entity that is characterized by consciousness and NON-MATERIALITY. We have already gained some insight into the significance of two of the key elements in this affirmation. Let us proceed to consider the third element, namely NON-MATERIALITY.

When we say that a spirit is a non-material entity, we give a negative description of spirit. For, in saying this, we are calling attention to what a spirit is NOT. In order to clarify this negative concept, we need to get clear concerning the nature of that which spirit is described as not being. In other words, we need initially to acquire clear thoughts concerning the nature of the material. What is *material* reality, i.e., matter? Let us consider in turn the main properties in terms of which materiality is definable.

To begin with, saying that a things is material in nature amounts to saying that it possesses magnitude, or bigness, in the sense of being "stretched out" in all directions. That is to say, a material thing is necessarily a something that has a definite size. The term which philosophers have most often employed for this in traditional discussions is "extension." So then, part of what we mean when we say that a thing is material in nature is that it is *extended*.

Next, to say that a thing is material in nature involves the claim that it has a shape. In philosophic discussions the term that is commonly employed is "figure." A material thing may be conceived of as successively assuming different shapes, or figures; however, at no time can it be conceived of as divesting itself of all shapes, or figures, whatsoever. Insofar as anything is material in nature, its materiality necessitates its possessing some shape or other, although not any particular shape.

Thirdly, the concept of a material thing is inseparably connected to that of space. That is, space-occupancy is a fundamental and indefeasible aspect of materiality. To be a material thing is necessarily to occupy space, and it is altogether inconceivable that a material thing could ever be otherwise than in space, at a definite location. To assert the contrary would be logically incompatible with the very concept of matter.

It will suffice to mention just one additional element in the notion of the material. Insofar as a thing is conceived of as being material, it is possible to conceive of that thing as being at rest, or as moving from place to place. Hence, the idea of mobility is an essential feature of the concept of materiality.

Now, if materiality consists in such things as size, shape, space-occupancy, and mobility, then NON-materiality consists simply in the absence of such properties. In other words, to say that something is non-material in nature amounts to saying that it is not characterized by such properties as size, shape, space-occupancy, and mobility.

Accordingly, to say that a spirit is a non-material entity is to say-- among other things--that a spirit is UNEXTENDED. Consistently with this, a spirit, unlike a material object, is not "stretched out" in all directions. A spirit, as a non-material entity, is--strictly speaking--neither small, nor large. Rather, the concept of magnitude, or size, simply does not apply to a spirit. By way of comparison, just as--strictly speaking--it is inappropriate to describe a sound as bright or dim, and just as it cannot rightly be said that a color is sweet or bitter, it is similarly impermissible to speak of a spiritual being as large or small. The point of this comparison is not to suggest that the same ontological categories are involved in all of these cases, but rather simply to underscore the *inapplicability* of the predicates "large" and "small" to spiritual beings. That is, the notion of literal extension is simply not an appropriate one in terms of which to talk about spirits.

Moreover, to say that a spirit is non-material is to assert that a spirit is a FIGURELESS entity. Consistently with this, a spiritual being, unlike a material object, does not have a shape. But, to say that a spirit is shapeless does not amount to the claim that a spirit is some sort of amorphous mass; rather, it is just to stress that a spirit has a nature such that it is entirely inappropriate to speak of it in terms of the notion of shape. Insofar as a spirit is figureless, in the sense required by its non-materiality, the concept of shape simply does not apply to it.

Furthermore, to say that a spirit is non-material implies that a spirit is a NON-SPATIAL entity. In keeping with this, a spirit cannot rightly be thought of as situated in any particular place. As non-material entities, spirits cannot be in space; for, to be in space is necessarily to possess size and shape, and the possession of size and shape is fundamentally incompatible with non-materiality. Again, insofar as a spirit is a non-material entity, it is simply inappropriate to speak of a spirit in terms of the idea of space.

Finally, the same considerations may be raised in connection with mobility. To say that spirits are non-material entities entails the claim that spirits are entities of a sort that cannot appropriately be spoken of as moving and being at rest. The only sense in which a spiritual being could rightly be thought of as moving is a metaphorical one; thus, a spirit may be conceived of as "moving" through different states of consciousness, successively. However, in the literal sense of moving from one point in space to another, or of being at rest in a particular location, the concept of mobility simply does not apply to spirits.

Careful and prolonged thought should be given to the various points that have been made regarding the spiritual. For, grasping the concept of the spiritual is not an easy task. An accurate understanding of what a spirit is would have to exclude all *sense-bound* thinking; and to accomplish such an exclusion may require sustained and strenuous exertion. A spirit is an ENTITY that is characterized by CONSCIOUSNESS and NON-MATERIALITY. That is the affirmation that was set forth at the outset of the present discussion. If we make a real effort to think our way into this affirmation, through a careful consideration of what has been said, then we shall succeed in lifting ourselves above purely sensual thinking, and arrive at a clear understanding of the concept of Spirit.

Before ending this section, let us briefly consider two terms that are closely related to the word "spirit." I refer to "soul" and "mind." The words "soul" and "mind" may be used as synonyms for "spirit." Thus, "soul" and "mind" can be defined in terms of what was said above concerning spirits. Nonetheless, selection of a certain one of these three words may sometimes indicate a desire on the part of the speaker to lay special emphasis on some particular aspect of a spirit's nature. For instance, the word "mind" is sometimes chosen with a view to calling special attention to the ordinary THINKING of a spiritual being; "soul" can be used in order to lay special stress on a spirit's FEELING nature; and "spirit" itself is sometimes employed with the aim of underscoring the fact of NON-MATERIALITY, or that of "higher," non-sensual THINKING (e.g., thinking concerning God and angels).

It goes without saying that the words "spirit," "soul," and "mind" are sometimes used in senses other than the one set forth above; for example, the word "mind" sometimes refers not to the underlying SUBJECT-of-consciousness, or thinkER, but rather to the CONTENTS-of-consciousness, or the THOUGHTS which belong to the thinkER. Nevertheless, the meaning that was previously explicated for "spirit," and which was subsequently extended to "soul" and "mind" is the one which has the greatest philosophico-religious importance. Moreover, in the remainder of this book the words "spirit," "soul," and "mind" will be used interchangeably; specifically, they will be used as signifying this: an ENTITY which is characterized by CONSCIOUSNESS and NON-MATERIALITY.

Some Consequences of the Idea<br>of Spirit

In the entire sphere, or range, of ordinary human experience there is only one thing which conforms to the account of Spirit presented above, namely what may be described as the innermost "I." That is, if we look deeply into what we mean when we utter the word "I," we shall see that the entity we are referring to, in making such an utterance, fully satisfies the definition of "Spirit" which was elaborated in the preceding discussion. Thus, one consequence of the characterization of Spirit presented above is that *the innermost"I" is a spirit.* That is, anyone who is able to utter the word "I," with genuine comprehension, is also able correctly to say: "I am a spirit." Moreover, for all who come to this recognition of the spirithood (or spiritual character) of the "I," the question of the existence of Spirit ceases to be in doubt; for, it is obvious that each one of us can say with absolute certainty, "I exist." That is, for each one of us, discernment of the spiritual nature of the innermost "I" renders the existence of Spirit as certain as our own existence.

The Latin word for "I" is "ego." Hence, if we take the word "ego," not in the popular sense of excessive vanity and pride, but rather in the sense of the original Latin, then, as an alternative to the above mode of expression, we may say that the innermost ego is a spirit. Moreover, for the sake' of brevity, we can use the word "ego," by itself, to refer specifically to the innermost "I." In this way we will avoid the necessity of having to add the adjective "innermost" to the word "ego" every time we use the latter.

Now, what exactly is the ego, or innermost "I?" There are many different ways of characterizing the ego which can contribute to the acquisition of clear thoughts concerning it. Let us consider three of them. First, it may be said that the ego is that which is retained as an object of awareness when--having initially focused awareness upon "self"--we then subtract from this awareness all consideration of a physical body. The requisite awareness may be attained equally effectively through either a self-contemplative act of ATTENTION, or a self-contemplative act of THINKING. Let us express this in the first person singular. If I first focus my *attention* upon "myself," and if I then wholly divert this attention away from my physical body, the ego is that which REMAINS as the object of my self-contemplative act of attention, even AFTER my physical body has thus been excluded from consideration. Moreover, if I first focus my thinking on my concept of myself, and then entirely remove from this conception all thought of a physical body, it is the concept of the ego, purely as such, that REMAINS as the object of this self-contemplative act of thought, even AFTER the idea of a physical body has thus been wholly removed.

It is possible that certain individuals will raise the following objection to what has been said here: This particular characterization of the ego does not assist me in the least in my effort to understand what the ego is; for, it seems to me that I just AM my physical body, and therefore, that--when I remove from my awareness all consideration of a physical body--there is nothing left in my awareness which could be referred to as "I." For the individual who is disposed to raise an objection such as this, the following two characterizations of the ego may prove to be more useful

A second way of characterizing the ego is this: The ego is that which endures throughout the different successive states of waking consciousness, as, so to speak, a STABLE CENTER. For, if we consider the course of ordinary waking experience, we see that there is a constant movement from one state of consciousness to another. There is an incessant coming-and-going of different states of seeing, different states of hearing, different states of feeling, and so forth. But, in the midst of this flux of experience, there is something which does NOT merely come-and-go, something which--unlike the passing sights, sounds, thoughts, and feelings--REMAINS in existence, without interruption, throughout the entire course of these passing states. Moreover, each of us is justified in making the pronouncement: "I myself AM this stable center; it is 'I' who go through these successive states." That is to say, the ego, the innermost "I," just IS the above described STABLE CENTER.

As a final characterization of the ego, we may say that the ego is the UNSEEN SEER of the various mental pictures which appear to us during the course of dream-consciousness. When we are immersed within the state of consciousness which is called "dreaming," it is certain that none of the "things" which we find in our dream-environment are actually physical objects, nor are any of these "things" strictly identical with the one who does the dreaming, i.e., the dreamer. During the course of a dream, we are "confronted," as it were, with *our own* inner condition, our own consciousness. Let us talk in terms of the second person singular.

None of the mental pictures which you "see" during a dream can rightly be said to be YOU YOURSELF. Imagine that, during your dream, you seem to yourself to be stretching out your arm, and to be looking at this outstretched arm. The dream-arm which you then "see" is certainly not you, nor is it even, strictly speaking, a part of you. The dream-arm is simply YOUR mental picture; it is merely one portion of the entire "visual field" which appears to you during your dream. Both the single mental picture, and this entire visual field *belong to* you, as modes of your own consciousness, just as waves belong to the lake on whose surface they are generated. But, what IS this "you," to which the dream-experiences belong? This "you" is the UNSEEN SEER of what appears in the dream; it is the "you" that SEES the dream-pictures, but which is not any one of the dream-pictures, nor any combination of such dream-pictures. This "you," rather, is the *owner* of the dream-pictures; while the latter are simply passing states which this "you" experiences. In other words, this "you" is you-your-very-self, you the EGO, or innermost "I." This shows the significance of characterizing the ego as the UNSEEN SEER of the mental pictures that appear during dream-consciousness.

A final observation needs to be made with respect to the last two characterizations of the ego presented above. It has been contended by some that there is no such thing as a SUBJECT-of-consciousness that is something different from passing STATES-of-consciousness. Here, the word "subject" means *something of which properties are predicated*, thus a property-POSSESSOR. According to this view, whenever we know, see, listen, and think, there is no underlying knowER that DOES the knowing, see-ER that DOES the seeing, listenER that DOES the listening, or thinkER that DOES the thinking; rather, on this view, there are only the passing knowledge-that-is-known, sights-that-are-seen, sounds-that-are-listened-to, and thoughts-that-are-thought. Briefly, this view maintains that passing states-of-consciousness do occur, but that there is no such thing as an underlying subject to which these passing states may be ascribed. This, for instance, is essentially the view propounded by the 18th century British philosopher David Hume--which view is called the "bundle theory" of the self. It is also the interpretation given by certain followers of Theravada Buddhism to the Buddha's teachings concerning *anatta*, i.e., "no-self."

Now, in response to objections along the lines of the above, it can only be said that gaining a genuine awareness of the ego is, in the last analysis, a matter of individual self-contemplation. That is, if--by means of sustained attention  and thought--we undertake to arrive at such self-contemplation, then it will become altogether clear that the ego is a reality. For, in this manner, we are able to arrive at a variety of self-awareness, in which we stand in a kind of direct confrontation with the ego, and in which its character as an underlying SUBJECT-of-consciousness is unmistakably discerned. Ultimately, then, there is no way in which--by using arguments--one individual can prove to another individual that the ego exists. Rather, each individual must establish this philosophically important point through an introspective investigation which seeks to discover this innermost "I."

The first consequence of the idea of Spirit may now be re-stated. It was said at the outset that one consequence that follows from the idea of Spirit is this: The ego, or innermost "I," is a spirit. In light of what has been said concerning the ego, it should now be clear to what extent this claim is justified. It was stated that a spirit is an ENTITY that is characterized by CONSCIOUSNESS and NON-MATERIALITY. If, now, unbiased consideration is given to the concept of the ego, it will be seen that the ego is wholly in conformity with this description of a spirit. Therefore, it may be said that the ego is a spirit. Moreover, since the ego--through introspective self-examination--is definitely to be met with within the sphere of ordinary human experience, it follows that Spirit is likewise accessible, in the course of such experience. In other words, this consequence runs counter to the widely held view that a spirit is some kind of MYSTERIOUS entity that is by no means to be encountered in the ordinary sphere of human life.

Another consequence of the idea of Spirit has to do with how we must understand phrases such as "my spirit," "my soul," and "my mind." The word "my" is ordinarily taken to imply that the thing to which it applies is something OTHER THAN I, or that I am something OTHER THAN IT. Thus, when I speak of my pen, my book, my car, etc., the word "my" is automatically taken to imply that the mentioned pen, book, and car are things other than I, or that I am something other than they. Similar considerations apply to the other possessive pronouns, e.g., "your," "his," "our," and so on. Nevertheless, it is a consequence of the idea of Spirit that "my" does NOT imply such otherness in the context of the phrase "my spirit." *My* spirit is not something other than I, which I merely possess. the phrase "my spirit" means the very spirit which *I am*. In this respect, the phrase "my spirit" is similar to the word "myself" (i.e., "my self"). *My* self is not something other than I, which I merely possess; rather, *my* self and I are one and the same. Exactly the same considerations apply to the two synonyms for "spirit," namely "soul" and "mind." *My* soul is not something other than I, but rather is simply I my very self. *My* mind, in the relevant sense, is not something other than I; rather, I and my mind are one and the same. The same points can be made with regard to the other possessive pronouns, when they are used with the words "spirit," "soul," and "mind."

A third consequence which follows from the idea of Spirit elaborated above is this: A spirit is a purely intelligible entity. In order to get clear concerning the significance of saying that a spirit is a purely intelligible entity, let us consider in turn the two components of the phrase "purely intelligible."

To say that a spirit is intelligible is to say that it is understandable, in the sense of being APPREHENSIBLE BY MEANS OF THOUGHT. In other words, the intelligibility of Spirit consists in the fact that we can have an awareness of the spiritual through THINKING. For, when we think correct thoughts concerning Spirit, this thinking is not merely a thinking-of-THOUGHTS-ABOUT-Spirit; rather, it is at the same an apprehending-of-SPIRIT-itself. In general, to think correctly about a thing is not only to think THOUGHTS, but also to apprehend the THING about which we think. Thus, in thinking correct thoughts about Spirit, we stand, so to speak, in the presence of Spirit and actually apprehend it; thinking and attending unite, as it were, into one mental operation. To say that a spirit is an intelligible entity, then, amounts to saying that a spirit can be thought about, and hence apprehended, in the manner indicated.

The other component of the phrase "purely intelligible" is "purely." When we add the word "purely," it is to underscore that spirits are apprehensible by means of thought ONLY. That is, to say that a spirit is a *purely* intelligible entity amounts to saying that a spirit cannot be directly apprehended by vision (or by any other sense-modality), and that consequently a spirit as such cannot be inwardly visualized (or in any way portrayed by concrete imagination). Thus, although Spirit is that which SEES, it cannot BE SEEN; and albeit Spirit is that which VISUALIZES, it cannot BE VISUALIZED. Nothing that we apprehend by means of our senses can possibly satisfy the definition of Spirit; and the same is true for any mental picture we might form through concrete imagination. At most, such things can only SYMBOLIZE Spirit, as light, for example, may be said to symbolize knowledge or warmth may be said to symbolize love. The purely intelligible nature of Spirit follows unavoidably from the fact of its NON-MATERIALITY.

Let us consider a fourth consequence of the idea of the spiritual. It was just stated that a spiritual being is necessarily a purely intelligible being. Nevertheless, there is a certain sense in which we may say that spirits can be seen. This sense is discoverable through following out the ramifications of the idea of Spirit. But, if--in a certain sense--spirits can be seen, then this sense would have to be one in which being seen would be compatible with being purely intelligible. So then, what exactly is this sense in which we may say that spirits can be seen? In order to clarify this, we need to recognize very clearly that an essential component of spirituality is PICTURE-MAKING POWER. That is, anything that satisfies the definition of Spirit is necessarily something which inherently possesses PICTURE-MAKING POWER. Picture-making power is simply that aspect of a spirit's POTENCY through which VISUALIZATIONS arise within it. In other words, picture-making power is that facet, or division, of spiritual POTENCY by means of which MENTAL PICTURES appear on the level of spiritual EXPRESSION. Briefly, it is the ability of spirits to experience color and form, and is the same power that gives rise to the mental pictures which we experience during dream-consciousness.

Now, let us suppose that the picture-making power of each spirit is such that it may give rise to visualizations which are extremely vivid. In fact, let us assume that--given appropriate conditions--the mental pictures which a spirit experiences, through this underlying power, may be so clear and intense that they are indistinguishable from the "things" we see in ordinary waking consciousness. Imagine, for example, that a dream-picture stood out in our dream-consciousness so distinctly, and with such intensity that it appeared to be in no way different from a so-called physical object. To take a specific case, suppose that you are in the midst of a dream-experience in which you seem to yourself to be standing in front of a tall oak tree; suppose, moreover, that the degree of vividness of this experience is such that all of the details of the dream-tree--its color, shape, and minute features--stand out in your consciousness with great clearness and strength. It is easy to concede that, by reason of such vividness the oak tree experienced in the dream would, in itself, appear to be in no way different from a "real" oak tree seen during waking-consciousness. It is vivid inner experience of this kind that we must assume spiritual beings to be capable of, when we ascribe to them picture-making power.

Another relevant point is that this picture-making power of spirits must be conceived of as both active and passive. Any given power is *active*, insofar as it comes to expression *without external inducement*; whereas, a power is *passive*, to the extent that it is brought to expression *by means* of external inducement. Let us use a comparison to illustrate. A body of water, say a lake, may be said inherently to possess WAVE-MAKING POWER. Every instance of an agitation, or disturbance, on the surface of a lake is an expression of this underlying power. If the lake were able to experience waves without any external inducement, then we would say that this wave-making power of the lake was an active power. In other words, if this wave-making power came to expression as actual wave-phenomena, without external inducement, then it would be an active power. However, insofar as the lake is able to experience waves by means of external inducement, its wave-making power is a passive one. For example, to the extent that this wave-making power of the lake is brought to expression through the action of wind--an external inducement--it must be said to be a passive power. So then, we can see the significance of saying that the picture-making power of spiritual beings is both active and passive. For, the picture-making power of a spiritual being is comparable to the wave-making power of a lake. The wave-making power of a lake is assumed to be an exclusively passive power; nevertheless, the meaning of "active power" can also be made clear through consideration of this example.

Now, let us focus on the spiritual being's passive ability to experience mental pictures; for, the possibility of spirits' seeing each other is based on this passive picture-making power. Think of two spiritual beings, each immersed in its own interior mental imagery. How can the one spirit "see" the other? The one spirit can "see" the other by means of SELF-REPRESENTATIVE IMPRESSIONS. This would involve a kind of *indirect* seeing. Let us attempt to see this point more clearly.

Let us refer to one of the above-mentioned spirits as "spirit A," and to the other as "spirit B." How can spirit A "see" spirit B? If spirit B makes an impression upon the inner consciousness of spirit A, and if this impression is representative of the existence and characteristics of spirit B, then spirit A may be said to "see" spirit B by means of a self-representative impression emanating from spirit B. This self-representative impression must be conceived of as a mental picture which spirit B induces on the consciousness of spirit A. Spirit A possesses *passive* picture-making power. And, in this case, we may suppose that the picture-making power of spirit A is brought to expression by a certain external inducement, namely the influence of spirit B's reality and character. Spirit A "sees" spirit B through a kind of influx which proceeds from the latter. Moreover, keeping in mind that spirit B is a multi-faceted reality, we may even conceive of a certain isomorphism between spirit B *per se*, and the self-representative impression which arises through spirit B within the consciousness of spirit A. In other words, it is possible to conceive of a kind of fixed correspondence between the various characteristics which spirit B intrinsically possesses and the several aspects of the mental picture which spirit B induces upon the consciousness of spirit A. For example, spirit B possesses the power of vision. Can this power of vision which belongs to spirit B appear within the consciousness of spirit A as "eyes" (i.e., as a mental picture of eyes)? Spirit B also possesses the power of hearing. Can this power of hearing which belongs intrinsically to spirit B appear within the consciousness of spirit A as "ears" (i.e., as a mental picture of ears)? Spirit B likewise possesses the power of smell. Can this power of smell which belongs to spirit B appear representatively within the consciousness of spirit A as a "nose" (i.e., as a mental picture of a nose)? Suppose that the total visual impression which spirit B makes upon the consciousness of spirit A has the "look" of a complete human body. Can every aspect of this mental picture of a complete human form be based on, or representative of, some *purely spiritual* characteristic of B? The assumption of an isomorphism of the sort described here would certainly be a useful hypothesis. For, throughout history, and in all cultures, there have been countless reports concerning so-called "apparitions." An apparition is what is popularly referred to as a "ghost." In the vast majority of such reports, the apparition, i.e., the discarnate spirit, is described as possessing a human form. To assume an isomorphism of the kind intimated above would help to explain this fact. Such an assumption would also be in keeping with numerous accounts contained in the scriptures of the major religions, in which spiritual beings (e.g., ancestors, angels, gods, etc.) are said to have been seen, as possessed of human form.

It is a clear implication of the concept of Spirit that each spiritual being must be thought of as a distinct center-of-consciousness, and as, so to speak, "closed off" within the boundaries of its own interior experience. Two spirits may be said to stand in a relation to one another which is similar to that of two persons who are sleeping in the same bedroom, where each person is deeply immersed within his/her own inner dream-consciousness and, so to speak, "cut off," or isolated, from the other person. However, there is nothing in the idea of Spirit which would prevent those things standing outside the boundaries of a spirit's consciousness from "entering" REPRESENTATIVELY into that spirit's consciousness. The spirit's own interior consciousness could, in other words, become the means by which external things are depicted, or representatively displayed to it.

Now, it is clear that what has been said concerning spirit B has equal applicability to spirit A. Spirit B could be said to "see" spirit A in the same sense in which spirit A was said to "see" B. Generally, it is a consequence of the idea of Spirit that spiritual beings may be conceived of as able to see each other by means of self-representative impressions.

A fifth consequence of the idea of Spirit is that spiritual beings, strictly speaking, must be conceived of as RACELESS. A spiritual being cannot correctly be said to belong to a race. But, it is possible to raise a certain objection to this claim. For, we noted in our discussion of the fourth consequence that spiritual beings can be conceived of as able to "see" each other. Is not color-experience inseparably bound up with seeing? If spirit A *sees* spirit B, is it not the case that spirit B must *appear*, within the consciousness of spirit A, as characterized by some definite color and other visual qualities? Does not the very faculty of vision itself require this? The answer to these questions is "yes." It follows from what was said previously that insofar as a spiritual being IS SEEN, it must appear as having a certain color and other visual qualities. Therefore, if race were simply a matter of such *appearing*, then it would have to be conceded that spiritual beings are characterized by race.

However, in support of the claim that spiritual beings are, in fact, raceless, it should be emphasized that race is an exclusively sensual concept. That is, race is wholly definable in terms of certain sense-perceptible qualities of individuals--e.g., qualities which we can directly see (i.e., color, facial features, etc.).

Now, as indicated, spiritual beings could certainly APPEAR to one another as characterized by various colors, and other corporeal features. However, such colors and corporeal features could not actually belong to the INTRINSIC nature of spiritual beings. A spiritual being, *per se*, simply cannot possess the kinds of characteristics in terms of which race is properly defined. Therefore, it must be said that a spirit, strictly speaking, cannot have a race, cannot belong to any particular racial group. Spiritual beings are necessarily RACELESS.

However, if we take the word "race" in a broad sense--a sense in which it is not restricted to the purely sensual--then it may be said that a spirit-being DOES have a race. In this broader sense of the word, the very spirituality, or spirithood, of a spirit may be said to constitute its race. Consistently with this, its status as an entity characterized by CONSCIOUSNESS and NON-MATERIALITY would determine its racial identity. Its power of vision, of hearing, of thinking, of feeling, and so on, constitute its racial characteristics. Thus, a sixth consequence following from the idea of Spirit is that all spiritual beings may be said to have a race. However, in this sense, they must all belong to ONE and the SAME race, namely the race of spirits.

A seventh consequence of the idea of Spirit has to do with the subject of gender. It is often simply taken for granted that a spiritual being must be either genderless, or somehow both masculine and feminine simultaneously. However, if we carefully reflect on the idea of gender, it will become clear that this assumption is not so obviously correct that we can simply take it for granted. For, it will be seen that gender, unlike race, is NOT primarily a sensual concept. Our conception of the male and of the female is not restricted to ideas derived from seeing, and other varieties of sense-experience. That is, in the degree that we gain CLARITY with respect to the idea of gender, and thereby come to RECOGNIZE that maleness and femaleness are not primarily sensual concepts, we will be able to see that there is nothing in the concept of Spirit which precludes the possibility that each spiritual being is characterized by a definite gender. In order to see more clearly that--from a purely conceptual standpoint--it is entirely permissible to think of each spiritual being as either inherently male, or inherently female, let us reflect on the following quotation from the philosopher Swedenborg:

> It is said that the masculine cannot be changed into feminine, nor the feminine into masculine, and that therefore after death the male is male; and the female is female; but as it is unknown in what the masculine and in what the feminine essentially consist, this shall here be briefly stated: The distinction consists essentially in the fact that in the male the inmost is love, and its vestment is wisdom, or what is the same, it is love overveiled with wisdom; and that in the female the inmost is that wisdom of the male, and its vestment is the love therefrom. But this love is feminine love, and is given by the Lord to the wife through the wisdom of the husband; and the former love is masculine love, and is the love of being wise, and is given by the Lord to the husband according to his reception of wisdom. It is from this that the male is the

wisdom of love; and that the female is the love of that wisdom. There is therefore, from creation, implanted in each a love of conjunction into one. ...In a word, nothing whatever is alike in them; and yet in the least things there is what is conjunctive. Nay, in the male the masculine is masculine in every even the least part of his body; and also in every idea of his thought, and in every particle of his affection. In like manner the feminine in the female. And as the one cannot therefore be changed into the other, it follows that the male is male, and the female is female after death.[1]

Now, this quotation admittedly contains many obscure pronouncements. However, this much at least seems clear: according to the above stated view, the male or female characteristics of a physical body are simply an outward expression of the inherent gender of the spiritual being who owns that particular body. Moreover, the above quotation declares not only that gender is *intrinsic to* spiritual beings, but also that gender is an *unchangeable* quality of each spiritual being. Furthermore, according to the account of gender set forth in this quotation, males, i.e., masculine spirits, and females, i.e., feminine spirits, have *in common* the faculties that constitute spirituality. Masculine and feminine spirits differ, not in terms of the particular faculties which they possess, but rather by virtue of *how* the faculties--which they have IN COMMON--*stand in relation to one another*, within each spirit. That is, in the masculine spirit the faculties of thinking and feeling stand inalterably in a certain relation to one another; whereas, in the feminine spirit the faculties of thinking and feeling stand indefeasibly in a relation to one another that is the reverse of that in which they stand in the masculine spirit. Moreover, this difference in the internal "arrangement" of spiritual faculties is clearly represented as rendering masculine and feminine spirits naturally suited for a special kind of union to one another.

Digressing for a moment, I wish to make use here of an analogy which occurs quite frequently in the writings of Abdu'l-Baha. And I utilize this analogy without in the least presuming to "interpret" the Baha'i scriptures. In *The Promulgation of Universal Peace*, Abdu'l-Baha states the following:

The world of humanity has two wings, as it were: One is the female; the other is the male. If one wing be defective, the strong perfect wing will not be capable of flight....

So long as these two wings are not equivalent in strength, the bird will not fly. Until womankind reaches the same degree as man, until she enjoys the same arena of activity, extraordinary attainment for humanity will not be realized; humanity cannot wing its way to heights of real attainment. When the two wings or parts become equivalent in strength, enjoying the same prerogatives, the flight of man will be exceedingly lofty and extraordinary.[2]

Using the rightness-leftness analogy invoked in the above quotation, let us make the following observations. The right wing and left wing of a bird are absolutely the same, with respect to their WING-HOOD; that is, each wing is just as much a wing as the other. But, despite this sameness of the two wings, the right wing and left wing are indefeasibly different, with respect to their SIDEDNESS, so to speak. The wing on the right side is essentially characterized by RIGHTNESS, and the wing on the left side is essentially possessed of LEFTNESS. If we were to remove a right wing and place it on the left side of the bird, this right wing would not thereby cease to have its character of rightness; in fact, it would not even properly "fit" on the left side. Similarly, a left wing superimposed upon the right side of the bird would not "fit," and would continue to be left in character just as it was before. In other words, right-wing-hood can never become left-wing-hood, nor can left-wing-hood become right-wing-hood. Nevertheless, right wings and left wings complement each other. Moreover, it is clear that two right wings do not complement one another in such a way as to make for efficient flight; nor is flight possible through the co-operation of two left wings. Efficient flight is rendered possible only through the mutually complementary action of a right wing and a left wing.

Now, let us take wing-hood as representing spirit-hood *per se*, and the rightness and leftness of wings as standing for the maleness and femaleness of spiritual beings. Consistently with this, we may say that precisely as each wing is just as much a wing as every other wing, so each spirit is just as much a spirit as every other spirit. There is absolute sameness on this level; this is the level of pure, universal person-hood as such. But, just as right wings and left wings may be regarded as inherently different with respect to their "sidedness," so also male spirits and female spirits may be viewed as essentially different with regard to their gender. On this view, the collective body of spirits, i.e., the entire community of spiritual beings, may be thought of as consisting of two sub-communities, one of these subcommunities being made up of male spirits, and the other of female spirits. Furthermore, the above quotation appears to subscribe to the idea that the true progress and well-being of the entire community of spirits is attainable only when the masculinity of those in the one sub-community, and the femininity of those in the other sub-community, are fully and *equally* unfolded; for, in this way the two sub-communities are rendered capable of co-operating in an optimal fashion, as mutually complementing segments of the universal spiritual community.

Thus, on the above view, each spirit may be referred to as "he" or "she." Nonetheless, if we wish, in a certain context, to mention spiritual beings without calling attention to the fact of gender, we are justified--within that context--in using the neuter pronoun "it" in reference to spiritual beings.

An eighth consequence is that all spiritual beings are possessors of boundless worth. For, if we unpack the full implications of the idea of spiritual POTENCY, we will discover that it is inseparably connected with the idea of unlimited goodness. As we think ever more deeply into the nature of Spirit, we are able to see with increasing clarity that Spirit--by reason of its potency--contains boundless opulence, namely the spiritual wealth of inexhaustible intelligence, kindness, fairness, generosity, patience, mercy, forbearance, courage, love, and so forth. Spiritual beings are boundlessly delightful and boundlessly fortunate. This is the significance of the claim that all spirits are possessors of boundless worth.

The ninth and final consequence which I will mention is this: In any community of spiritual beings absolute egalitarianism must obtain. That is, not only is it the case that spiritual beings possess worth, it is also the case that they must all possesses EQUAL worth. For, the worth of spirits is determined by their very spirituality, or spirithood, *per se*, and this cannot differ from one spirit to another. However much spirits might differ in the manner and degree of their MANIFESTATION of spirituality, they can never differ among themselves in terms of the fundamental POSSESSION of spirituality. Thus, for example, it is not conceptually permissible for us to say that one spiritual being could essentially POSSESS more intelligence than some other spiritual being (But, it *is* possible that, at certain point time, one spiritual being might REVEAL more intelligence than another.) For, intelligence is an aspect of spirituality, as such. It cannot differ among spiritual beings, or be lacking in some of them, any more than wetness can differ among drops of water, or be lacking in some of them. Accordingly, absolute egalitarianism is an inescapable consequence of the concept of Spirit. Furthermore, in order to avoid possible misconceptions, it should be explicitly stated that this absolute egalitarianism fully obtains in connection with masculine souls and feminine souls. In other words, if the previously mentioned consequence regarding gender is rightly understood, then it will be seen to be in complete harmony with the principle of equality. An inherent, spirit-based distinction of gender, such as that delineated above, does not in any way allow for the conclusion that masculine souls are superior to feminine souls, or conversely, that feminine souls are superior to masculine souls; such inequality between the sexes is totally precluded by the very concept of spirit itself.

To recapitulate, from the idea of Spirit it follows that: (1) The ego, or innermost "I," is a spiritual being; (2) The phrases "my spirit," "my soul," and "my mind" mean *I my very self*; (3) Spiritual beings are purely intelligible; (4) Spiritual beings may be conceived of as able to "see" each other; (5) Strictly speaking, spiritual beings have no race; (6) In a looser sense of the word "race," all spiritual beings belong to ONE race; (7) It is logically permissible to think of spiritual beings as inherently possessing gender; (8) Due to their potency, all spiritual beings are characterized by boundless worth, or dignity; and (9) All spiritual beings are equal in fundamental worth, or dignity.

## What Do We Mean "Life After Death"?

Let us attempt to get clear about the significance of the question "Is there life after death?" To raise this question obviously amounts to asking the following: Do we continue to be *alive*, after we have become *dead*? But when we explicitly put the question in this way, it exhibits a decidedly paradoxical character. For, clearly, the words "alive" and "dead" are opposite in meaning; "dead" means *not-alive*. Thus, we could re-formulate the original question as follows: Do we continue to be alive after we have become "not-alive"? In that case, it would seem that giving an affirmative answer to this question amounts to the self - contradictory claim that we do continue to be alive at the very time when we have become not-alive. Viewing the matter in this way, to ask the question "Is there life after death?" would seem as pointless as to ask whether there is any such thing as a circular square. But this is surely not the correct way in which to view the matter. Let us examine the notion of life after death more carefully.

In order to grasp the concept of life after death in the right manner, we need to take cognizance of two altogether distinct conceptions of life. (A third way of using the words "life" and "death" is based on the notions of *connection* and *disconnection*, and will be discussed later.) That is, we need to distinguish between two different senses of the word "life"; and, we need similarly to distinguish between two different senses of the corresponding adjective "alive." For, on the one hand, there is what may be referred to as *physiological* life, and, on the other, what can be called *mental* life. In the physiological sense of the word, life consists in such things as breathing, the beating of the heart, the electro-chemical activity of the brain, and the various intra-cellular activities of the body (i.e., the diverse processes that go on within individual cells). However, mental life consists in such things as thinking, understanding, feeling, desiring, visualizing, loving, hating, color-sensations, sound-sensations, and so forth. To express the point in general terms, we may say that mental life consists in consciousness, with all of its various modes-of-manifestation. Moreover, even if one were to claim that mental life somehow DEPENDS ON physiological life (or conversely, that phys- iological life somehow DEPENDS ON mental life), nonetheless, strictly speaking, it is not the case that physiological life and mental life are one and the same. For, each has a distinct nature incompatible with the other. It is certain that the expressions "physiological life" and "mental life" designate two wholly different concepts.

Now, the question "Is there life after death?" ceases to seem paradox- ical, when we interpret it in light of the above distinction. More, specif- ically, to ask if there is life after death amounts to asking: Do we somehow continue to be alive MENTALLY, even after we have become not-alive PHYSIOLOGICALLY? In other words, do we continue to be alive as mental beings even after our physiological life has ceased, or come to end?

There are obviously just two possible answers to this question; that is, broadly speaking, the answer must be either "yes" or "no." Let us call the affirmative answer the "survival theory," and let us refer to the negative answer as the "annihilation theory." The survival theory, then, asserts that we do in fact continue to be alive as mental beings, even after our physiological life has ended; while, the annihilation theory--the idea that to die is to be reduced to absolute NOTHINGNESS--maintains that we do not continue to be alive as mental beings after physiological life has ended. Now, varying forms of the latter view, i.e., the annihilation theory, are not possible. However, it is possible to distinguish between numerous varieties, or versions, of the former theory. The remainder of this chapter will be devoted to enumerating some of the major forms which the survival theory may assume.

Each variety of the survival theory to be considered will be expounded in terms of the answers which it gives to the following questions: (1) In the last analysis, what are we, that is, what does our personal identity truly consist in? (2) What is it that principally differentiates the period called "life" from that which commences at the point of physical death? (3) What is death in the specific sense of an event, that is, what is DYING? and (4) What is death in the specific sense of an outcome, that is, what is BEING DEAD? As we shall see, most varieties of the survival theory agree in the answers they give for questions 1, 2, and 3. They are distinguishable as separate varieties of the survival theory primarily on the basis of the different answers they give to question 4.

## The Simple Disembodiment Theory

The view which is designated here as the "simple disembodiment theory," may be defined in terms of the following core assumptions: (1) Persons are spiritual beings, not physical bodies; (2) During "life," persons maintain a certain connection with a physical body; (3) As it pertains to persons, *dying* is simply disconnection from the physical body. In other words, when we die we are disconnected from the physical body to which we were connected during "life"; and (4) As it pertains to persons, *being dead* is simply a PERMANENT condition of bodiless existence. That is, after the person has been fully disconnected from the physical body, the resulting state of "disembodiment" continues indefinitely.

Extending back to very ancient times, the simple disembodiment theory has been held within many different cultures. What mainly sets it apart from other forms of the survival theory is the belief that the bodiless existence assumed to characterize persons after death is an enduring state of affairs. Strictly speaking, there is no supposition of any sort of "return." Persons are viewed as purely spiritual beings, whose existence is neither impaired, nor diminished by disconnection from the physical body.

As an instance of the many different cultural settings within which this view is found, let us consider the case of African traditional religion. Professor E.B. Idowu, a well-known specialist in the field of African religion, states the following:

The specific belief of the Yoruba about those who depart from this world is that once they have entered After-Life, there *they remain*, and there the survivors and their children after them can keep unbroken intercourse with them, especially if they have been good persons while on earth and were ripe for death when they died.' In fact, the place where the ancestors live *permanently* is the 'paradise' for which Africans yearn as their *final* home--a 'heaven' in which they have a happy, unending reunion with their folk who are waiting for them on the other side. The belief of the Dahomeans will be an illuminating example in this connection: when a person leaves this earth, he makes a *final* journey to the after-life. He crosses over three rivers, and clambers up a mountain to reach the valley where his forebears live.³

## The Reincarnation Theory

The core assumptions of the theory of reincarnation are the following: (1) Persons are spiritual beings, not physical bodies; (2) During "life," persons maintain a certain connection to a physical body; (3) As it pertains to persons, dying is simply disconnection from the physical body; and (4) As it pertains to persons, being dead is simply a TEMPORARY condition of bodiless existence, which, sooner or later, is followed by re-entrance into a physical body, through ordinary physical conception and birth. Again, what differentiates the reincarnation theory from other varieties of the survival theory is what it asserts concerning the situation into which a person is placed as a result of dying. This theory regards the normal process of birth as, so to speak, a "gate" through which disembodied persons may *repeatedly* come back into connection with a physical body. There are at least four distinguishable versions of the reincarnation theory, namely (1) transmigration, (2) palingenesis, (3) partial reincarnation, and (4) spiritual descent. Let us briefly consider each of these varieties of reincarnationism, in turn.

The transmigration version of this theory is distinguished from the other three views by the supposition that it is possible for souls to incarnate as animals even if--in their previous life--they were incarnated as human beings. For example, if we interpret literally certain statements attributed to Socrates in the writings of Plato, then it would appear that Socrates subscribed to this view. In the following passage from the *Phaedo* Socrates describes the differing destinies of souls after their separation from the physical body:

'I mean, for example, that those who have trained themselves in gluttony, unchastity and drunkenness, instead of carefully avoiding them, will naturally join the company of donkeys or some such creatures, will they not?'
'Yes, very naturally.'
'Whereas those who have set more value upon injuring and plundering and tyrannising over their fellows will join the wolves and hawks and kites. Or should we give such souls as these some other destination?'
'By no means,' said Cebes; 'leave them where you have put them.'
'Then it is obvious, I take it, where all the other types will go conformably to the roles in which they have severally trained themselves.'
'Quite obvious, I agree.'
'Now is we may call any of these happy, the happiest, who pass to the most favoured region, are they that have practiced the common virtues of social life, what are called temperance and justice, and virtues which spring from habit and training devoid of philosophic wisdom.'
'Why are they the happiest?'
'Because they will naturally find themselves in another well-conducted society resembling their old one, a society of bees, per-

haps, or wasps or ants; and later on they may rejoin the human race they have left, and turn into respectable men.'
'Naturally enough.'
'But the society of gods none shall join who has not sought wisdom and departed wholly pure; only the lover of knowledge may go thither. And that is the reason, dear friends, why true philosophers abstain from the desires of the body, standing firm and never surrendering to them; they are not troubled about poverty and loss of estate like the common lover of riches; nor yet is their abstinence due to fear of the dishonour and disgrace that attach to an evil life, the fear felt by the lovers of power and position.'[4]

In opposition to the transmigrationist view, the paligenesis variety of reincarnation theory (from the Greek: palin = again; and genesis = production) denies that a soul that was previously incarnated as a human being can subsequently incarnate as an animal. That is, according to the palingenesis view, a soul that lives as a human being, and then abandons its physical body at death, cannot "come back" as an animal in its future incarnation. The Hindu thinker, Sri Aurobindo, takes this position in the following quotation:

We arrive then necessarily at this conclusion that human birth is a term at which the soul must arrive in a long succession of rebirths and that it has had for its previous and preparatory terms in the succession the lower forms of life upon earth; it has passed through the whole chain that life has strung in the physical universe on the basis of the body, the physical principle. Then the farther question arises whether, humanity once attained, this succession of rebirths still continues and, if so, how, by what series or by what alternations. And, first, we have to ask whether the soul, having once arrived at humanity, can go back to the animal life and body, a retrogression which the old popular theories of transmigration have supposed to be an ordinary movement. It seems impossible that it should so go back with any entirety, and for this reason that the transit from animal to human life means a decisive conversion of consciousness, quite as decisive as the conversion of the vital consciousness of the plant into the mental consciousness of the animal. It is surely impossible that a conversion so decisive made by Nature should be reversed by the soul and the decision of the spirit within her come, as it were, to naught.[5]

The idea of partial reincarnation is found most notably within the context of African traditional religion. According to this view, departed souls do in fact re-incarnate (i.e., they do re-enter into connection with bodies through physical birth); however, this re-incarnating involves a kind of spiritual influx such as need not deprive them of their status as inhabitants of the supersensible realm. In other words, while remaining established in the afterlife as a spiritual being, an individual soul is somehow enabled to project itself "downward" to the physical plane, and thereby, to impress its own nature, or soul qualities, upon one or more of its descendants. Consider the following quotations:

> Belief in reincarnation is reported among many African societies. This is, however, partial reincarnation in the sense that only some human features or characteristics of the living-dead are said to be "reborn" in some children. This happens chiefly in the circle of one's family and relatives. The living-dead who has been reincarnated continues, however, to have his separate existence and does not cease to be.[6]

> Nevertheless, we find ourselves confronted with the paradox involved in the belief of the Yoruba that the deceased persons do 'reincarnate' in their grandchildren and great-grandchildren. In the first place, it is believed that in spite of this reincarnation, the deceased continue to live in After-Life; those who are still in the world can have communion with them, and they are there with all their ancestral qualities unimpaired. Secondly, it is believed that they do 'reincarnate,' not only in one grandchild or great-grandchild, but also in several contemporary grandchildren and great - grandchildren who are brothers and sisters and cousins, aunts and nephews, uncles and nieces *ad infinitum*. Yet, in spite of these repeated 'rebirths'..., the deceased contrive to remain in full life and vigour in the After-Life.[7]

According to the spiritual descent version of the reincarnation theory, discarnate spiritual beings are able to reincarnate in the specific sense of sometimes "coming down" into a position *within* the supersensible world, from which they can interact and co-operate with selected persons who still live in physical bodies. Through forming a special link with the "living" person, the discarnate soul is able to inspire and assist the former in the attainment of certain ends toward which they both aspire. Although he only rarely uses the word "reincarnation," the Reverend Sun Myung Moon gives an admirably clear statement of this view in his book entitled *Divine Principle*:

> Also, the spirit men who left their missions unaccomplished on earth descend to earthly men whose missions are similar to those with which the spirit men were charged while on earth, and cooperate with them for the accomplishment of the will. Seen from the standpoint of mission, the physical body of the earthly man serves as the body of the spirit man. The earthly man, receiving the cooperation of the spirit man, would accomplish the mission of the spirit man as well as his own.... Accordingly, these spirit men descend to earthly men of their choice and, by cooperating with them, accomplish the mission which they left unfulfilled in their earthly lives. Therefore, the earthly man, receiving the cooperation of the spirit man, is the second coming of that spirit man, he also appears to be the reincarnation of the spirit man.... The doctrine of reincarnation, upheld by Buddhism, comes from an interpretation of external appearances, without knowing the theory of "resurrection through second coming."[8]

In the above quotation it is said that the earthly man APPEARS to be the reincarnation of the spirit man. What is the significance of using the word "appears"? It is this: The earthly man only APPEARS to be the reincarnation of the spirit man in the sense of transmigration, palingenesis, or partial reincarnation, but the earthly man actually IS the reincarnation of the spirit man in the sense of spiritual descent.

### The Resurrection Theory

Our English word "resurrection" is derived from the Latin "re" and "surgere," which mean *again* and *rise*, respectively. Moreover, consistently with this etymological point, the common thread that runs through the various forms of the resurrection theory is the idea of *rising again*. But, in order for something to rise, there must first obtain some sort of state of abasement, or fallen condition, from which the rising can proceed. In other words, only that which is somehow fallen can engage in the act of rising; or, if any given thing is NOT fallen, then it cannot rise. Therefore, it is worth noting here that the notion of resurrection is inseparably tied to the idea of a prior state of abasement.

In what follows we shall consider four different versions of the resurrection theory, namely (1) the corporalist view, (2) the interim-disembodiment view, (3) the monadological view, and (4) the spiritual quickening view.

The corporalist version of the resurrection theory, strictly speaking, is not a form of the survival theory. For, in reality, it advances the idea of REvival, not SURvival. Its core assumptions are the following: (1) Personal identity is wholly understandable in terms of the physical body. In other words, persons *just are* appropriately functioning physical bodies, and nothing more; (2) Since, a person is nothing more than a physical body, to say that a person is alive, is simply to say that a certain physical body is alive, i.e., that a certain physical body *is functioning*. In other words, a *living* person is simply a physical body that exhibits breathing, heart-beat, brain-activity, etc.; (3) Dying is simply the cessation of the body's functioning. That is, a person's dying consists in the stopping of respiration, heart-beat, brain-activity, and so forth; (4) The outcome of dying, namely *being dead*, has two major phases. The first phase is characterized by the mere absence of vital functions; the person is DEAD in that the physical body (which IS the person) no longer exhibits breathing, heart-beat, brain-activity, etc. The second phase consists in non-existence. For, even though in the early period following death we may still speak of a dead PERSON, the gradual process of decomposition that commences at the outset of that period eventually reaches a point at which we are no longer justified in so speaking. The person has been ANNIHILATED. At this point, neither a living person, nor a dead person any longer exists. Henceforth, we may rightly speak of the existence of dust, cremation-ashes, etc., but not of the existence of a person. But, in spite of this non-existence of the person, God will in the future miraculously intervene in the natural course of things, and will effect a re-creation of the person, and a restoration of the person to full vital functioning. This miraculous intervention is to occur at a definite time in the future, variously referred to as "the Day of Judgment," "the Second Coming of Christ," "the Day of Resurrection," etc.

For example, the corporalist version of resurrection theory would appear to be the one referred to in the following quotation from the *Encyclopaedia Judaica* (1971):

> The belief that ultimately the dead will be revived in their bodies and live again on earth is a major tenet of Judaism.... This idea has been taken so seriously and literally that pious Jews are often concerned about the clothes they are buried in, the complete interment of all organs, and being buried in Israel.[9]

The interim-disembodiment version of the resurrection theory maintains the following: (1) Persons are spiritual beings, not physical bodies; (2) During "life," persons maintain a certain connection with a physical body; (3) As it pertains to persons, dying is simply disconnection from the physical body; and (4) As it pertains to persons, being dead is simply a TEMPORARY condition of bodiless existence, which will come to an end when--on Judgment Day, the Second Coming of Christ, or the Day of Resurrection--a miraculous intervention of God brings about a re-creation of physical bodies (somehow spiritualized and improved), and a re-connection of discarnate persons with those re-created bodies. But, in the interim, i.e., in the meantime between death and resurrection, discarnate persons await the re-acquisition of their bodies in a purely spiritual world, e.g., "heaven" or "paradise."

There is a passage from the *Tragic Sense of Life*, by Miguel de Unamuno, in which the interim-disembodiment view is very clearly expounded:

> "With the same bodies and souls that they had," as the Catechism says. So much so that it is orthodox Catholic doctrine that the happiness of the blessed is not perfectly complete until they recover their bodies. They lament in heaven, says our Brother Pedro Malon de Chaide of the Order of St. Augustine, a Spaniard and a Basque, and "this lament springs from their not being perfectly whole in heaven, for only the soul is there; and although they cannot suffer, because they see God, in whom they unspeakably delight, yet with all this it appears that they are not wholly

content. They will be so when they are clothed with their own bodies."[10]

It is possible to distinguish a third variety of the resurrection theory, namely what may be called the "monadological view." I have chosen the adjective "monadological" to describe    this position, because it is based on the general metaphysical theory known as "monadological pluralism." Among philosophers who have subscribed to this type of world-view the best-known is probably Gottfried Leibniz (A.D. 1646-1716). The monadological pluralist position amounts to a kind of *spiritual* atomism. According to this conception, the entire universe is nothing but a vast multitude of single, indivisible entities which, to stress their singleness, are called "monads" (Greek, monas = one), and which, to underscore their indivisibility are called "true atoms" (Greek, atomos = uncuttable). All of these monads, or spiritual atoms, are conceived of as in process of evolution from a dim and confused condition of consciousness to one that is progressively more intense and distinct. However, they are thought to undergo this evolution at differing rates. Thus, at any given point in time some of these spiritual atoms are assumed to be in a sleep-like stage of development, and some highly "awake," while others are at various intermediate stages in the development of their consciousness. On this view, what is called the human "ego" is simply one of these monads (or spiritual atoms) which has progressed to a highly advanced stage in the evolution of its consciousness; that is, the human ego is a highly awakened monad. On the other hand, the human body, in itself, is nothing but a large GROUP of comparatively undeveloped monads, monads that still slumber at a lower stage in the evolution of their consciousness. That is, a single highly awakened "atom" (the human ego) is thought to enter into a special connection with a certain group of sleeping "atoms," and by reason of this special connection, the latter (i.e., the group) is referred to as the body of the former.

Now, with the above as its basic metaphysical position, the monadological variety of the resurrection theory asserts the following: (1) A person is a single spirit (i.e., ONE monad or spiritual atom) which has attained a comparatively advanced stage of consciousness. Thus, each person is something *other than* the group of slumbering monads which constitute the body of that person; (2) During "life," each person maintains a certain connection with that large group of monads which constitute the body of that person; (3) As it pertains to persons, dying is simply disconnection from the body (i.e., disconnection of the single developed monad from the group of undeveloped monads which were its body); and (4) As it pertains to persons, the outcome of dying is a PERMANENT condition of bodiless existence; however, each of the slumbering monads which were previously the "body" of the now bodiless person *will continue to undergo evolution*, and will eventually advance to the stage of a fully awakened person. Thus, the resurrection of the body is simply the process of evolution which brings about this gradual awakening of the spiritual atoms which, at one time, served as the body of a more advanced spiritual being.

I do not wish to suggest that Leibniz himself subscribed to what I have called the "monadological version" of resurrection theory; it is entirely possible that Leibniz himself was not even aware of these ramifications of his basic position. Nonetheless, it is certain that, if we assume the correctness of a spiritual atomism such as that which Leibniz propounded, then resurrection can be conceived of along the lines set forth above. Reflection on the following quotation from H.W. Carr's book on Leibniz will shed further light on the metaphysical view on which the monadological conception of resurrection is based. The last statement in this quotation is especially noteworthy:

> The three kinds of monads (the bare monads, the animal monads, and the rational monads) are never conceived by Leibniz as constituting exclusive classes. Not only is there a hierarchy, but there is an infinite gradation and there is no limit to the possibility of a monad rising in the hierarchy. The lowest has within it the potentiality of the highest.... One of his commentators (Gottlieb Hanschius, quoted by Condillac in a note to his *Traite des Systemes*) tells the story that Leibniz remarked to him once, while taking coffee, "There may be in this cup a monad which will one day be a rational soul."[11]

With respect to personal identity, being alive, and dying, the spiritual quickening version of the resurrection theory is fundamentally in agreement with most other forms of the survival theory. That is, the spiritual quickening view maintains that persons are *other than* bodies, that being alive involves a certain *connection with* the body, and that dying involves *disconnection from* the body. However, as regards the

OUTCOME of dying, spiritual quickening embraces a distinctive position. According to the spiritual quickening view, what dying ultimately leads to is not a resurrection of the physical body; rather, the word "resurrection" applies exclusively to the spirit. We are to be resurrected as purely spiritual beings. The word "quick" is a synonym for "alive"; thus, to quicken something is to enliven it, or to confer more abundant life upon it. The spiritual quickening view maintains that resurrection is a process in which spiritual beings receive a more abundant measure of life; it is assumed to consist in a kind of intensification or enrichment of the interior life which a spirit can manifest. According to this view, when spiritual beings are resurrected, they experience a significant heightening of the various facets of their consciousness; thus, the expression of picture-making power, of intelligence, of attention, of emotion, and of the other modes of consciousness is substantially strengthened. Some advocates of this view believe that the resurrection occurs for each person, individually, at the moment of physical death. But, on this view, resurrection is not necessarily a single, instantnaeous event; on the contrary, it may also be conceived of as a gradual process, extending over a long period of time. In fact, since the interior life of spiritual beings must be conceived of as capable of endless unfoldment, resurrection, in this sense, would seem to be a process which may continue indefinitely. Below are some passages from the writings of Baha'u'llah, founder of the Baha'i Faith. These passages present an account of the soul's experiences after death which is in keeping with the spiritual quickening version of the resurrection theory. Referring to the soul he states:

> And now concerning thy question regarding the soul of man and its survival after death. Know thou of a truth that the soul, after its separation from the body, will continue to progress until it attaineth the presence of God, in a state and condition which neither the revolution of ages and centuries, nor the changes and chances of this world can alter.

> Consider the lamp which is hidden under a bushel. Though its light be shining, yet its radiance is concealed from men. Likewise, consider the sun which hath been obscured by the clouds. Observe how its splendor appeareth to have diminished, when in reality the source of that light hath remained unchanged. The soul of man should be likened unto this sun, and all things on earth should be

regarded as his body. So long as no external impediment inter-
veneth between them, the body will, in its entirety, continue to
reflect the light of the soul, and to be sustained by its power. As
soon as, however, a veil interposeth itself between them, the
brightness of that light seemeth to lessen.

When it leaveth the body, however, it will evince such ascendancy,
and reveal such influence as no force on earth can equal. Every
pure, every refined and sanctified soul will be endowed with tremendous power, and shall rejoice with exceeding gladness.[12]

Consistently with the above, we may conceive of the process of
resurrection as including: (1) the spiritual development which takes place
prior to "death"; (2) the sudden intensification and enrichment of interior
life that occurs immediately after "death," that is, which occurs upon the
soul's release from the hindering influence of the body; and (3) the
progressive quickening, or gradual enhancement, of consciousness which
continues indefinitely after death. (In the Baha'i Faith, the term
"resurrection" is believed to have a wide range of different meanings;
however, the meaning which is pertinent to the present discussion is the
one set forth above.)

To recapitulate, we have discussed a total of nine different forms of
the survival theory, namely (1) the simple disembodiment view, (2) the
transmigrationist view of reincarnation, (3) the palingenesis view of
reincarnation, (4) the partial reincarnation view, (5) the spiritual descent
view of reincarnation, (6) the corporalist view of resurrection, (7) the
interim-disembodiment view of resurrection, (8) the monadological view
of resurrection, and (9) the spiritual quickening view of resurrection.

## Inter-Religious Harmony?

Now, the broad categories under which the various forms of the
survival theory have been subsumed are these three: The Simple
Disembodiment Theory, The Reincarnation Theory, and The Resurrection
Theory. The various religious traditions of the world, for the most part,
advocate some form of one or another of these three broad views. Let us
divide the major religions of the world into four main groups: (1) primal
religions, (2) religions of Far Eastern origin, (3) religions of Indian
origin, and (4) religions of Middle Eastern origin. Primal religions

include those traditions which arose within so-called primitive cultures, and without the benefit of sacred writings, e.g., African traditional and Native American religions. Religions of Far Eastern origin include Taoism, Confucianism, and Shintoism. Religions of Indian origin include Hinduism, Buddhism, and Jainism. And religions of Middle Eastern origin include primarily Judaism, Christianity, and Islam.

Now, within both primal religions and those of Far Eastern origin, the prevailing view of survival is that of simple disembodiment. But, within religions of Indian origin the dominant view is that of reincarnation; while in those of Middle Eastern origin the theory of resurrection is universally endorsed.

I would like to end this chapter by calling attention to the following point. Simple disembodiment, reincarnation as spiritual descent, and resurrection as spiritual quickening are mutually compatible conceptions of survival. Therefore, if these three forms of the survival theory gain wide acceptance within the various traditions, a significant step in the direction of inter-religious harmony will have been made. Adoption of certain other forms of the reincarnation and resurrection theories would also be conducive to such harmony. I have mentioned just this one instance, for the sake of brevity. In any event, assuming the legitimacy of the 9-point universalist perspective referred to at the beginning of this book, we should expect that an intensive study of the scriptures of the various religions would lead to the discovery of mutually consistent views of life after death.

*Notes*

[1]Warren, S.M. (ed.), *A Compendium of the Theological Writings of Emanuel Swedenborg* (New York: Swedenborg Foundation, 1977), pp. 443-444.
[2]Abdu'l-Baha, *The Promulgation of Universal Peace* (Wilmette: Baha'i Publishing Trust, 1982), pp. 174 and 375.
[3]Idowu, E.B., *Olodumare: God in Yoruba Belief* (Essex, England: Longmans, 1962), p. 194. (Emphasis added.)
[3]Idowu, E.B., *African Traditional Religion* (Maryknoll, New York: Orbis Books, 1975), pp. 188-189. (Emphasis added.)

[4]Hackforth, R. (trans.), *Plato' Phaedo* (Cambridge: University Press, 1973), pp. 89-90.
[5]McDermott, Robert (ed.), *The Essential Aurobindo* (New York: Schocken Books, 1974), pp. 102-103.
[6]Mbiti, J.S., *African Religions and Philosophy* (New York: Doubleday, 1970), p. 215.
[7]Idowu, E.B., *African Traditional Religion* (New York: Orbis Books, 1975), pp. 187-188.
[8]Moon, S.M., *Divine Principle* (New York: HSA-UWC, 1977), pp. 187-188.
[9]*Encyclopaedia Judaica* (1971). Quoted in *The Watchtower*, June 15, 1989, p. 5.
[10]Unamuno, Miguel de, *Tragic Sense of Life* (New York: Dover, 1954), p. 66. [11]Carr, H.W., *Leibniz*, (New York: Dover Publications, 1960), p. 179.
[12]*Gleanings from the Writings of Baha'u'llah* (Wilmette, Illinois: Baha'i Publishing Trust, 1976), pp. 154-155.

CHAPTER SIX:


PROVING LIFE AFTER DEATH

CHAPTER SIX: Proving Life After Death

In the present chapter several distinct lines of argumentation in support of the survival theory will be considered. In each of these attempts at proving life after death the concept of Spirit figures centrally; consequently, an accurate assessment of them depends on the possession of clear thoughts concerning Spirit. The explication of the concept of Spirit carried out in the previous chapter brings out the crucial points that need to be grasped; thus, sustained consideration of these points is requisite, if the following arguments are to be seen as in any degree plausible. Furthermore, it should be borne in mind that--in the present discussion--the words "soul" and "spirit" will be used as synonyms.

## The Simplicity Argument

The first argument that we shall examine has had numerous proponents, and dates back to extremely ancient times. Let us call it the "simplicity argument" for survival. The crucial premise in this argument is the claim that each spiritual being is an indivisible unit. One of the earliest written expressions of this argument is found in Plato's dialogue, the *Phaedo*, which was written in the fourth century before the birth of Christ. In the following quotation from this dialogue the main speaker is the philosopher Socrates:

Socrates then resumed: "Now the sort of question that we ought to put to ourselves is this: what kind of thing is in fact liable to undergo this dispersal that you speak of? For what kind of thing should we fear that it may be dispersed, and for what kind of thing should we not? And next we should consider to which kind the soul belongs, and so find some ground for confidence or for apprehension about our own souls. Am I right?"

"Yes, you are."
"Well now, isn't anything that has been compounded or has a composite nature liable to be split up into its component parts? Isn't it incomposite things alone that can possibly be exempt from that?"
"I agree that that is so," replied Cebes.....
"Well then, that being so, isn't it right and proper for the body to be quickly destroyed, but for the soul to be altogether indestructible, or nearly so?"
"Certainly."[1]

As a second illustrative instance, I cite a passage from Abdu'l-Baha's *The Promulgation of Universal Peace*. Describing the human soul as "the inner and essential reality of man," Abdu'l-Baha gives the following, extremely clear presentation of the simplicity argument:

Every composition is necessarily subject to destruction or disintegration. For instance, this flower is a composition of various elements; its decomposition is inevitable. When this composed form undergoes decomposition--in other words, when these elements separate and disintegrate--that is what we call the death of the flower. For inasmuch as it is composed of single elements, the grouping of multitudinous cellular atoms, it is subject to disintegration. This is the mortality of the flower. Similarly, the body of man is composed of various elements. This composition of the elements has been given life. When these elements disintegrate, life disappears, and that is death. Existence in the various planes, or kingdoms, implies composition; and nonexistence, or death, is decomposition.
But the inner and essential reality of man is not composed of elements and, therefore, cannot be decomposed. It is not an elemental composition subject to disintegration or death. A true and fundamental scientific principle is that

an element itself never dies and cannot be destroyed for the reason that it is single and not composed.[2]

In our attempt to clarify and assess the simplicity argument, let us use the following reconstruction:

PART I
(1) Premise: That which is genuinely simple can never be destroyed.
(2) Premise: Spiritual beings are genuinely simple.
CONCLUSION: Therefore, spiritual beings can never be destroyed.
PART II
(1) Premise: As established in PART I above, spiritual beings can never be destroyed.
(2) Premise: Persons are spiritual beings.
CONCLUSION: Therefore, persons can never be destroyed.

Let us focus on PART I of the above reconstruction. We need to raise at least two separate questions with respect to its first premise: (a) What is the significance of describing something as "genuinely simple"? and (b) What is the meaning of "destroyed"? In other words, once we have arrived at a clear apprehension of the concept of simplicity, and of that of destruction, we should be in a position to ascertain to what extent it is plausible to say that the simple cannot be destroyed. We shall look into the notion of simplicity first.

Within the context of the present discussion, the word "simple" is a synonym for "non-composite." Moreover, in order to gain clarity on the concept of the non-composite, we obviously must first get clear as to the corresponding affirmative concept, i.e., that of the composite. Consequently, in our effort to achieve clarity concerning the notion of the simple, we may begin with a consideration of the opposing idea of the composite.

Now, noting that the word "composite" can be used both as an adjective and as a noun, let us ask: What exactly is a composite? The meaning of this term is evident from its etymology; it is derived from the Latin words "cum" and "ponere," which signify, respectively, *together* (or *with*) and *to put*. Thus, on the etymological meaning of the word, a composite is something that is *put together*. Moreover, the word "composite," as it is currently employed in English, has retained this original meaning. More explicitly, by "composite" is meant *anything that is made up of MANY elements which have been PUT TOGETHER so as to form ONE*. The key portions of this account of the composite are "many elements," "put together," and "to form one." The first two of these are sufficiently clear, but what is the significance of the third? What precisely are we to understand by the claim that the elements going into the make-up of a composite are put together in such a way as to form ONE? Two possible answers suggest themselves. Let us consider these two possibilities in turn.

One possibility is that many elements, when they are "put together" to form a composite, actually become ONE thing. On this view, the discrete elements that go into the make-up of any given composite literally lose their separate identities as a result of the formation of that composite. That is, elements which, prior to being composed, were MANY single entities CEASE TO BE MANY through the process of composition, that is to say, are totally merged into ONE thing. Let us refer to this as the "mergerist view" of composites, since it assumes that elements actually *merge*. Now, if this conception of composites is correct, then no element which goes into the make-up of a given composite can rightly be said to retain its individual identity (i.e., its existence as a distinct entity), when once that composite has been formed. But, what evidence is there to support such a view of composites?

The strongest evidence in favor of this view is provided by ordinary sense-experience. For, the various objects that appear to us through the functioning of our senses are undoubtedly composites; and each of these composites is experienced as a solid and unitary thing, as if all of its component elements have MERGED into ONE thing. Take, for instance, the human body. When we engage in what is called "looking at" another person, what presents itself to the visual sense is experienced as a solid, or unbroken, expanse; in other words, we see the human body as a single continuum spread out in our visual field. It seems to be all-in-one-piece, so to speak. Therefore, according to the testimony of the sense of sight, all of the discrete elements that entered into the formation of the human body have MERGED into ONE thing. According to the representation which is given to us through our visual sense, the elements that went into the make-up of the human body have NOT retained their separate identities; rather, they have lost their existence as distinct things, due to the formation of the composite human body. Such is the testimony of the senses. But, we may ask at this point: Are the sensory appearances in keeping with reality? A host of reasons could be adduced to show that the answer to this question is "no."

Let us focus again on the human body. If we could observe the human body with the aid of a specially constructed and extremely high-powered microscope, what appears to the naked eye as "all one piece" would be seen rather as a vast multitude of distinct entities, each separated from the others by a great distance. Furthermore, if this microscope were sufficiently high-powered to allow observation of the *ultimate* "elementary particles" which supposedly make up the human body, then it would be seen that each of these ultimate components of the body *retains its individual identity and character*, even after the composite human body has been formed. In other words, the "putting together" of these elements does not cause them to lose their existence as single entities; consequently, after they have been brought together to form the human body, they remain just as much a MULTITUDE, just as much MANY, as when--prior to composition--they were scattered throughout a wide portion of the earth. The upshot of these remarks is that single elements have a stable identity, which is in no way interrupted through processes of composition and dissolution, but rather remains intact throughout both.

It is clear what the above considerations imply with regard to the mergerist view of composites which we set out to examine. That view maintains that many elements, when they are "put together" to form a composite, actually become ONE thing (not merely in appearance, but IN REALITY). It seems certain from what we have noted above that this mergerist view of composites is wrong. But, what is the alternative? How must we formulate a correct account of composites? I shall briefly address this matter in what follows.

First, I submit that even though every composite is portrayed by the visual sense-modality as "all in one piece," that is, even though we *see* each composite as ONE thing, nonetheless, every composite is in reality a GROUP of things. Every composite is actually a MULTITUDE of entities, in which each single entity retains its own separate existence, despite having been "put together with" other entities to form a composite. Each element in a composite may indeed be somehow under the influence of the other elements in that composite, that is, the state or condition of each element may be largely determined by the character and presence of the other elements in that composite. However, the fact of such mutual influence would in no way imply a loss of their separate identities, or a cessation of their existence as distinct individuals.

Consistently with the various points that have been made, I wish to put forward the following account of composites. A composite is a GROUP of things which--as a result of the putting together, and consequent mutual proximity of its separate members--APPEARS to the visual sense as "all in one piece." This formulation presupposes the use of "composite" as a noun. But, if we wished to underscore the adjectival use of this word, we could say the following: By "composite" is meant *consisting of MANY single elements, which have been "put together" in such great proximity to on another, that they APPEAR to the visual sense as ONE thing, but each of which IN REALITY continues to exist as a distinct entity.* For convenience, we may refer to this alternative view as the "non-mergerist view" of composites; for on this view, the elements of composition never actually merge but, rather, always retain their status as separate entities.

Now that we have gotten clear concerning composites, let us turn to a consideration of the corresponding negative concept, i.e., that of the non-composite. For, we want to clarify the notion of the simple, and, as stated previously, "simple" means *non-composite*. If the meaning of "composite," briefly put, is *consisting of MANY*, then the meaning of "non-composite" is obviously just the negation of this. Succinctly stated, "non-composite" means *not consisting of many*. Moreover, the description "not consisting of many" implies the description "consisting of exactly ONE." (This, of course, is to discount the description "consisting of exactly zero things," and it should go without saying that small quantities such as two or three would also be subsumed under the description "many.") Accordingly, the result we arrive at is this: To say that something is "genuinely simple" is to say that that something in reality amounts to exactly ONE thing, and thus that it is not a multitude of things merely appearing to be one through being closely conjoined to each other.

We have now adequately addressed the first question we raised concerning the simplicity argument, namely the question "What is the meaning of 'genuinely simple'?" The second question was this: What is the meaning of "destroyed"? From the passages cited at the outset of this chapter, it is clear that proponents of the simplicity argument subscribe to what could be called a "dispersalist view" of destruction. Etymologically speaking, to disperse something is to *scatter apart* (Latin: "dis" = apart, and "spargere" = to scatter). Thus, according to the dispersalist view of destruction, to destroy a thing is just to scatter apart its component elements, or, at the very least, to alter significantly the arrangement of those elements. For example, if we were to place a set of marbles on a floor in a certain three-sided configuration, we could speak of the existence of a triangle. If subsequently we scatter the marbles over the floor, or at least significantly alter their arrangement, then we could rightly speak of this as the *destruction* of the triangle. The dispersalist view of destruction maintains that all instances of destruction are similar to this case of the triangle. That is, on this view, to destroy a thing is invariably nothing more than to scatter, or disarrange, its component elements.

But, is the dispersalist view of destruction correct? From a purely empirical standpoint, it would seem that all cases of the destruction of things, which we encounter in ordinary life can, in fact, be understood in terms of the scattering or disarrangement of minute parts. Take, for instance, a wooden table. What would the destruction of this table really amount to? If we were to grind the entire table into sawdust, that certainly would involve the destruction of the table. However, let us keep in mind the particulate structure of this table. If the table could be viewed microscopically, what appears to the naked eye as "one piece" would be discovered to be in reality a multitude of elementary particles. If we were to destroy the table by grinding it into sawdust, this destruction of the table could obviously be understood in terms of the disarrangement of its grosser components. So, it is clear that this example does conform to that of the scattered marbles.

But, what if we were to burn this sawdust to the point of bare ashes, and allowed the wind to scatter these ashes throughout the world? Would not this result in the complete annihilation of what was previously a table? That is, could we not say that what was previously a table is now wholly NONEXISTENT? For, obviously, the ashes have now VANISHED, that is, we no longer see them. And, as far as the five senses are concerned, this would indeed SEEM TO BE a complete annihilation of what was previously the table. Nevertheless, it would surely be a mistake to say that what was previously the table is now wholly non-existent. For, not even one of that multitude of elementary particles which formerly made up the table has ceased to exist, as a result of what we have done. If our power of vision were somehow rendered microscopically acute, we would be able to see that each of the elementary particles which formerly made up the table, and which subsequently existed as sawdust and ashes, continues its individual existence intact, even after the ashes have entirely vanished from sight. These elements of the table have merely been so widely dispersed that they no longer make an IMPRESSION on our visual sense; in other words, our visual consciousness has merely ceased to register, or represent, this group of particles as a sensuous picture. Briefly, we no longer "see" it. But these now widely dispersed particles are the very same entities which at one time were arranged in such a way as to appear through vision as a single expanse. Initially these elements were arranged in a way that resulted in their being called "a table." Later, this arrangement was altered in such a way that they came to be described as "sawdust." And finally, their arrangement became such that they appeared to the visual sense as a "pile of ashes." Accordingly, although the elements of the table have been widely scattered, they have not been annihilated, they have not become non-existent. We may conclude, then, that this instance also is in conformity with the scattered-marbles example. More generally speaking, all of the points which have been made in these two cases involving the destruction of the table are also applicable to every conceivable case of destruction as encountered in ordinary sense-experience. Hence, we may infer that the dispersalist view of destruction--at least from the standpoint of the senses--is correct.

Let us return now to the simplicity argument for survival. More specifically, let us focus again on premise (1) of PART I of the reconstruction set forth earlier. Premise (1) says: That which is genuinely simple can never be destroyed. We are now in a position to state definitively that this premise of the argument is correct. That is, the simplicity argument is wholly justified in its claim that the simple cannot be destroyed. For, as we previously noted, to say that something is genuinely simple is to say that that something in reality amounts to exactly ONE thing, and to say that something has been destroyed is to say that the component elements of that something have been significantly scattered or disarranged. But, that which amounts to exactly ONE thing has no component elements which could be scattered or disarranged. It follows that the simple--since it is exactly ONE thing, and hence, has no component elements--cannot undergo any scattering or disarrangement as to component elements, which is to say, it cannot be destroyed. Consequently, premise (1) of the simplicity argument is true.

Next, let us look at premise (2) of the reconstruction. Premise (2) states that spiritual beings are genuinely simple. The key concepts utilized in this proposition, viz., "spiritual beings" and "genuinely simple," should be clear from previous discussion. But, what rational justification can be adduced in support of this claim? What basis do we have for saying that spiritual beings are genuinely simple? I wish to offer the following argument:

PART I
(1) Premise: If any given thing possesses a uniform quality, then--if this thing is composite--it must consist of numerous parts, each one of which possesses that same quality which the thing as a whole uniformly possesses.
(2) Premise: Every spiritual being possesses a uniform quality, namely the quality of KNOWING.
CONCLUSION: Therefore, if spiritual beings are composites, then a spiritual being consists of numerous parts, each one of which possesses that same quality, i.e., KNOWING, which a spiritual being as a whole uniformly possesses.
PART II
(1) Premise: As established in PART I above, if spiritual beings are composites, then a spiritual being consists of numerous parts, each one of which possesses that same quality, i.c., KNOWING, which a spiritual being as a whole uniformly possesses.
(2) Premise: But, it is NOT the case that a spiritual being consists of numerous parts, each one of which possesses that same quality of KNOWING, which a spiritual being as a whole uniformly possesses.
CONCLUSION: Therefore, it is NOT the case that spiritual beings are composites.

To avoid confusing it with the simplicity argument itself, let us refer to the above as the "ancillary argument." In order to get clear concerning this ancillary argument, we need first of all to see what is meant by "uniform quality." To say that a thing possesses a uniform quality amounts to saying that the thing in question possesses that quality IN ITS ENTIRE BEING. To say that a given thing possesses some quality *uniformly* is to say that it has that quality THROUGHOUT, that that quality constitutes its GENERAL CHARACTER. Take, for example, the common conception of a material thing. (For present purposes, it is not important whether or not something corresponding to this conception actually exists; we need only recognize the possibility of conceiving, or *thinking about*, such a thing.) Imagine a specific material thing, say, a large grapefruit. As we consider this grapefruit, let us ask ourselves: From among its various qualities, is there any one quality which the grapefruit possesses IN ITS ENTIRE BEING? Is there any one of the grapefruit's qualities which constitutes its GENERAL CHARACTER? If we adopt the ordinary view of material things, we may say that the grapefruit clearly does have such a quality. Using the verb "to extend" in its intransitive sense, we may say that IN ITS ENTIRE BEING the grapefruit *extends*, i.e., that it possesses the quality of EXTENDING. For, the grapefruit is characterized by magnitude, or size, and its size consists in the fact of its extending, "stretching out," in every direction. In other words, this quality of extending constitutes the GENERAL CHARACTER of the grapefruit. This example illustrates in a clear fashion what is meant here by "uniform quality" in the ancillary argument. Let us proceed now to an assessment of this argument. Even a superficial look at the ancillary argument is sufficient to show that PARTS I and II are both valid in form. Thus, we need only to focus on the individual premises of the argument, in order to determine whether or not it is sound.

The first premise of PART I states the following: If any given thing possesses a UNIFORM QUALITY, then--if this thing is a composite--it must consist of numerous parts, each one of which possesses that same quality which the thing as a whole uniformly possesses. To clarify, the significance of this premise, let us return to the grapefruit example. As we just noted, the grapefruit may be said to possess a UNIFORM QUALITY, namely the quality of EXTENDING. Let it be further noted that the grapefruit is definitely a composite. For, even though its parts are normally thought to be mutually contiguous, it does, nonetheless, have numerous distinguishable parts. For instance, we may distinguish an upper hemisphere, a lower hemisphere, a right hemisphere, and a left hemisphere, just to mention some of its grosser parts. Now, from the fact that this grapefruit has EXTENDING as its uniform quality, and at the same time is composite, it follows that this grapefruit consists of numerous parts, each of which possesses that same quality, namely EXTENDING, which the grapefruit as a whole uniformly possesses. Hence, from the fact that the grapefruit as a whole uniformly possesses the quality of EXTENDING, it follows that the upper hemisphere also EXTENDS; that lower hemisphere likewise EXTENDS; that the right hemisphere similarly EXTENDS; and that the left hemisphere EXTENDS as well. The same considerations apply to all of the other parts which constitute the composite being of the grapefruit. That is, the uniformity of the grapefruit's quality of EXTENDING has the consequence that each one of its parts also

EXTENDS. So then, the point of premise (1) is to make the more general claim that precisely parallel observations would have to be made in connection with *every* COMPOSITE which possesses a UNIFORM QUALITY. Consequently, it may be inferred that premise (1) is true.

Now, let us assume that each spiritual being is a composite. In that case, it would follow from the above that if each spiritual being possesses a UNIFORM QUALITY, then each spiritual being consists of numerous parts, and every one of these parts possesses this same quality. But, is it in fact the case that a spiritual being is the possessor of a UNIFORM QUALITY? In the second premise of PART I, this is exactly what the ancillary argument claims. In order to see clearly that this second premise is true, we must understand the nature of Spirit; specifically, we must recognize that each of us finds an example of Spirit in the ego, the innermost "I." Insofar as I am able to contemplate myself as an ego, it becomes clear to me that I am an entity characterized by consciousness and non-materiality. And in consequence of this realization I come to the understanding that I MYSELF AM a spiritual being. Hence, in attending to, and reflecting on, my own true nature, I am in fact attending to, and reflecting on, the nature of a spiritual being.

The important thing to note here is that such individual self-contemplation reveals that the "I," a spiritual being, does possess a UNIFORM QUALITY, namely the quality of CONSCIOUSNESS. Or, taking the word "knowing" in its most inclusive sense (i.e., as a synonym for "consciousness"), we may say that individual self-contemplation reveals the fact that the "I," a spiritual being, uniformly possesses the quality of KNOWING. That is, as I consider my own nature, I discover that IN MY ENTIRE BEING I possess that quality of KNOWING. Accordingly, just as the afore-mentioned grapefruit was said to be an EXTENDER with respect to its whole nature, so similarly I recognize myself to be a KNOWER with respect to my whole nature. This implies that the second premise of PART I is correct.

But let us be altogether clear as to what this means. Use of the grapefruit example will facilitate our task, since it provides us with a visualizable comparison. It was stated earlier that since the grapefruit is uniformly characterized by extension, each of its numerous parts must also be characterized by extension. Thus, the right hemisphere EXTENDS; the left hemisphere EXTENDS; and so forth for all of the parts of the composite grapefruit. Now, if spiritual beings are composites, then the fact of each spirit's UNIFORMLY possessing the quality of KNOWING forces us to say things concerning each of its parts which parallel the things we said concerning the parts of the grapefruit. Thus, if each spirit UNIFORMLY possesses the quality of KNOWING, if, in other words, each spirit IN ITS ENTIRE BEING is a KNOWER, then we are compelled to say that a spirit must consist of numerous parts, every one of which possesses that same quality of KNOWING which a spirit as a whole uniformly possesses. In other words, if spirits are NOT genuinely simple, but rather consist of parts, then all of the numerous parts of a spirit must be KNOWERS, just as all of the numerous parts of a grapefruit are EXTENDERS; each part of a spirit would have to be just as truly a CONSCIOUS ENTITY as a spirit in its composite wholeness. This is the significance of the conditional statement which occurs as the conclusion in PART I of the ancillary argument.

Let us proceed to PART II of the ancillary argument. The conditional statement that was established as the conclusion of PART I now reappears as the first premise of PART II. Hence, in examining PART II, we may by-pass premise (1) and go directly to the second premise of the argument. Briefly expressed, premise (2) amounts to the claim that a spiritual being does not consist of MANY knowers. But how can we be sure that this is true? By means of individual self-contemplation what we have called the ego, i.e., the innermost "I," reveals itself to be a spiritual being, and also to be exactly ONE knower. Thus, for example, when I consider the ego which I myself amount to, I not only discern my own nature as a spiritual being (i.e., recognize my status as an entity characterized by consciousness and non-materiality), I also clearly apprehend that I am exactly ONE knower. That is, when I focus my attention and thought on what I am with respect to the WHOLE of my being, I discover that I do not consist of MANY knowers. For, if I consisted of MANY knowers, then in the very act of clearly apprehending the WHOLE of myself, I would also necessarily take awareness of the MANY knowers of which I consisted.

It goes without saying that the thought-experiment which I have just outlined must be performed by each individual for himself/herself. However, I submit that if the appropriate introspection and reflection are carried out in an unbiased fashion, then the truth of the statement "A spiritual being does not consist of many knowers" will be clearly seen. Consequently, we are justified in regarding premise (2) as a true statement.

The final conclusion of the ancillary argument is this: Spiritual beings are not composites. Thus, since the form of both parts of this argument is clearly valid, and since all of its premises make plausible claims, we are justified in concluding that the ancillary argument is sound. And if that is the case, then it follows that spiritual beings are NOT composites. Moreover, to say that spiritual beings are not composites amounts to the claim that spiritual beings are indeed genuinely simple.

Let us return now to the simplicity argument itself. PART I of this argument, as previously reconstructed, advances the claim that spiritual beings are genuinely simple. This claim appears as premise (2) of PART I. Accordingly, we are now in a position to say that premise (2) is a true statement. Moreover, since PART I is obviously valid in form, and since both of its premises have now been shown to be plausible, it follows that PART I of the simplicity argument may be regarded as sound. Therefore, the conclusion that spiritual beings can never be destroyed would appear to be correct.

As for PART II of the simplicity argument, its first premise may be taken as having already been established as the conclusion of PART I. Consequently, the main purpose of PART II is merely to make an explicit connection--through premise (2)--between persons and spiritual beings; its aim is to stress that persons (i.e., we ourselves) *just are* spiritual beings. Moreover, in order to see clearly that this identification of persons with spiritual beings is justified, the various points set forth in Chapter 5 should be carefully reviewed.

The final conclusion of the simplicity argument is that persons can never be destroyed, that is to say, that *we ourselves* can never be destroyed; this is equivalent to saying that the survival theory is correct. Furthermore, since all the premises of the simplicity argument may be regarded as true, and since both of its sub-arguments are valid in form, it follows that this argument for survival is sound.

Nonetheless, there is a certain objection which can still be raised against this argument. For, the simplicity argument acknowledges only those cases of destruction which involve dispersal of the elements of a thing. But, what if we conceive of destruction not as the scattering or disarrangement of parts, but rather in terms of an instantaneous, total cessation of existence? A thing's being simple certainly would prevent it from being subject to destruction by dispersal, but mere simplicity, as such, is not sufficient to preserve a thing from destruction, conceived of as instantaneous utter annihilation. The second argument for survival which we shall consider has the advantage that in seeking to prove that persons can never be destroyed, it understands "destroyed" specifically as meaning *utterly annihilated.*

### The Substance Argument

The next argument which we shall consider may be called   the "substance argument" for life after death. For an early statement of this argument, let us again turn to the writings of Plato:

> Now a first principle cannot come into being, for while anything that comes to be must come to be from a first principle, the latter itself cannot come to be from anything whatsoever; if it did, it would cease any longer to be a first principle. Furthermore, since it does not come into being, it must be imperishable, for assuredly if a first principle were to be destroyed, nothing could come to be out of it, nor could anything bring the principle itself back into existence, seeing that a first principle is needed for anything to come into being.
> The self-mover, then, is the first principle of motion, and it is as impossible that it should be destroyed as that it should come into being: were it otherwise, the whole universe, the whole of that which comes to be would collapse into immobility, and never find another source of motion to bring it back into being.
> And now that we have seen that that which is moved by itself is immortal, we shall feel no scruple in affirming that precisely that is the essence and definition of soul, to wit, self-motion. Any body that has an external source of motion is soulless, but a body deriving its motion from a source within itself is animate or besouled, which implies that the nature of soul is what has been said.
> And if this last assertion is correct, namely that 'that which moves itself' is precisely identifiable with soul, it must follow that soul is not born and does not die.[3]

The writings of Abdu'l-Baha provide us with another instance of this argument:

> Some think that the body is the substance and exists by itself, and that the spirit is accidental and depends upon the substance of the body, although, on the contrary, the rational soul is the substance, and the body depends upon it. If the accident--that is to say, the body--be destroyed, the substance, the spirit, remains.
> Second, the rational soul, meaning the human spirit, does not descend into the body--that is to say, it does not enter it, for descent and entrance are characteristics of bodies, and the rational soul is exempt from this. The spirit never entered this body, so in quitting it, it will not be in need of an abiding-place: no, the spirit is connected with the body, as this light is with this mirror. When the mirror is clear and perfect, the light of the lamp will be apparent in it, and when the mirror becomes covered with dust or breaks, the light will disappear.
> The rational soul--that is to say, the human spirit--has neither entered this body nor existed through it; so after the disintegration of the composition of the body, how should it be in need of a substance through which it may exist?[4]

Extracting the essential points of the above quotations, we may reconstruct the substance argument as follows:

PART I
(1) Premise: Anything that is a true substance can never be destroyed.
(2) Premise: Each spiritual being is a true substance.
CONCLUSION: Therefore, a spiritual being can never be destroyed.

PART II
(1) Premise: As established in PART I above, a spiritual being can never be destroyed.
(2) Premise: Persons are spiritual beings.
CONCLUSION: Therefore, persons can never be destroyed.

Let us start with the premise: Anything that is a true substance can never be destroyed. Why should we accept this premise as true? In order to see the plausibility of this premise, we need to be altogether clear about the term "substance." The philosophic sense of this term, to which I alluded earlier, is the one intended here. Thus, we should not understand "substance"--in this context--as equivalent to "material stuff." Rather, by "substance" is meant *that which is able to engage in DOING* (whether this be *active* DOING or *passive* DOING), that is, *anything which is able to GO THROUGH different states successively, and which does not at any time lose either its existence or essential character in the process.* This philosophic sense of the word "substance" is wholly in keeping with the etymology of the word. "Substance" is derived from the Latin words "sub" · (beneath) and "stare" (to stand). Thus, a substance is something which STANDS BENEATH; it is that which remains constant at the center of change. The notion of *beneath* is a means of indicating that substance is that which SUPPORTS the process of change. And the concept of *standing* is a way of conveying the idea that substance is that which PERSISTS in the midst of such change, i.e., RETAINS ITS EXISTENCE AND ESSENTIAL CHARACTER throughout all instances of undergoing change.

This can be illustrated by means of a concrete case. Let us make use of the clay-example that was employed earlier, since that is easy to visualize. In this example we say that the clay undergoes change from one condition to another, but that the clay, as such, remains the same throughout the process of changing. By *abstracting* from this example, we can take hold of the pure concept of substance, wholly severed from any conception of material things.

Now, it should be noted that this account implies that a substance by definition can never be destroyed. In other words, the very nature of a substance precludes the possibility that a substance could be destroyed. For, anything which satisfied the definition of "substance" would have to persist throughout EVERY instance of changing. Thus, if it turned out that some particular thing, X, was destroyed in the course of a certain process of change, it would follow that X was in fact *not* a substance. It follows, therefore, that premise (1) is doubtless true. But to admit that a substance, by definition, can never be destroyed is not necessarily to accept that any such thing as a substance actually exists. On the contrary, to make this admission is only to concede a *conceptual* point, namely this: The concept of substance is such that *if* something actually exists corresponding to this concept, then that something can never be destroyed. Accordingly, the question to ask is: What reason do we have to believe that anything corresponding to the idea of substance actually does exist? More specifically, why should we accept premise (2), PART I, as true? Let us try to determine whether or not there is rational justification for saying that a spiritual being is a substance. The following argument purports to show that spiritual beings are substances:

(1) Premise: Anything which can actually engage in DOING, that is, can GO THROUGH different states successively is a true substance.
(2) Premise: A spiritual being can actually engage in DOING, that is, a spiritual being can actually GO THROUGH different states successively.
CONCLUSION: Therefore, a spiritual being is a true substance.

Thus, according to the above argument, spiritual beings may be said to be substances because of the fact that they actually engage in a certain kind of DOING. More specifically, spiritual beings are able to engage in *mental* DOING. A spiritual being is able to GO THROUGH different states-of-*consciousness* successively. Thus, for example, I, a spiritual being, find that I can engage in *mental* DOING, both actively and passively. I can actively go through different states-of-mental-picturing, or visualizing; I can actively go through different states-of-thinking; I can passively go through different states-of-dream-consciousness; and I can passively go through different states-of-sense-experience. Moreover, I note that I myself, a spiritual being, invariably persist in the midst of these alternating states-of-consciousness. Consequently, since the ego (or innermost "I") endures as the center of such mental changing, and since the ego just is a spiritual being, it follows that a spiritual being is a true substance. Therefore, returning to PART I of the substance argument, we are now in a position to say that its second premise is also true. Indeed, the reasoning set forth in PART I seems cogent. Moreover, since PART II, again, simply makes the connection between persons and spirits, it may be inferred that the substance argument as a whole does succeed in establishing its conclusion.

## The Argument from Apparitions

Let us now turn to a third argument for survival, one less purely philosophical in character. This third argument belongs to the category of so-called "empirical" arguments for life after death. We may call it the "argument from apparitions." As we had occasion to note previously, an apparition is what is popularly referred to as a "ghost." Throughout history claims concerning apparitions have been made by many different individuals. However, the most extensive efforts at collecting, and systematically documenting, such accounts seem to have been made during the 19th and early 20th centuries. The classic work *Human Personality and its Survival of Bodily Death*, by F.W.H. Myers is particularly noteworthy in this regard, and also for adducing many other varieties of empirical evidence in favor of survival. Of the many cases reported by Myers, one of the better-known is that of a certain travelling salesman who "saw" an apparition of his sister, who had died nearly ten years earlier. This is supposed to have occurred in a hotel room in St. Joseph, Missouri, as the salesman sat working on orders he had received. In his own words:

> "I suddenly became conscious that some one was sitting on my left, with one arm resting on the table. Quick as a flash I turned and distinctly saw the form of my dead sister, and for a brief second or so looked her squarely in the face; and so sure was I that it was she, that I sprang forward in delight calling her by name, and, as I did so, the apparition instantly vanished...I was near enough to touch her...and noted her features, expression, and details of dress, etc. She appeared as alive."[5]

Another case is reported by the philosopher C.J. Ducasse in his book *The Belief in a Life After Death*:

> The case was that of the numerous apparitions at the beginning of the 19th century of the form of the deceased Mrs. Butler in a Maine village, to which the Rev. Abraham Cummings (A.M. Brown University 1776) had proceeded in order to expose what he had assumed must be a hoax. He, however, was then himself met in a field by what he terms "the Spectre." His statement of this meeting reads: "Sometime in July 1806, in the evening I was informed by two persons that they had just seen the Spectre in the field. About ten minutes after, I went out, not to see a miracle, for I believed that they had been mistaken. Looking toward an eminence, twelve rods distance from the house, I saw there, as I supposed, one of the white rocks. This confirmed my opinion of their spectre, and I paid no more attention to it. Three minutes after, I accidentally looked in the same direction, and the white rock was in the air; its form a complete Globe, white with a tincture of red, like the damask rose, and its diameter about two feet. Fully satisfied that this was nothing

ordinary, I went toward it for more accurate examination. While my eye was constantly upon it, I went on four or five steps, when it came to me from the distance of eleven rods, as quick as lightning, and instantly assumed a personal form with a female dress; but did not appear taller than a girl seven years old. While I looked upon her, I said in my mind, 'you are not tall enough for the woman who has so frequently appeared among us!' Immediately she grew up as large and as tall as I considered that woman to be. Now she appeared glorious. On her head was the representation of the sun diffusing the luminous, rectilinear rays every way to the ground. Through the rays I saw the personal form and the woman's dress."[6]

One thing that is especially notable about the above case is that it involves an apparition which allegedly was seen by many different persons, both simultaneously and successively. Professor Ducasse goes on to make the following observations:

...the Rev. Mr. Cummings reproduces some thirty affidavits which he had obtained at the time from persons who had seen or/and heard the Spectre; for the apparition spoke, and delivered discourses sometimes over an hour long.... It presented itself sometimes "to one alone....sometimes she appeared to two or three; then to five or six; then to ten or twelve; again to twenty; and once to more than forty witnesses. She appeared...several times in the open field...There, white as the light, she moved like a cloud above the ground in personal form and magnitude, and in the presence of more than forty people. She tarried with them till after daylight, and vanished."[7]

We have looked at only two cases here, but there is an enormous amount of material dealing with other, similar cases. Undoubtedly, some of these accounts could be the result of hallucinations, or even of outright fraud. However, no genuinely unbiased investigator, who sufficiently examines this literature is likely to conclude that ALL of these reports can be dismissed as such. Moreover, the argument from apparitions presupposes that there is no other plausible explanation for such reports apart from that provided by the survival theory. This argument for survival may be worded simply as follows:

(1) Premise:   If there were no life after death, then apparition-sightings would not be extensively reported.

(2) Premise:   But, apparition-sightings are, in fact, extensively reported.

CONCLUSION:  Therefore, there is life after death.

But, how can we be sure that there is no OTHER means of explaining apparition-reports (that is, apart from assuming the continued existence of deceased persons)?  Even if we can definitely rule out hallucinations and fraud as explanations, how can we be certain that positing the survival of persons after death is the ONLY way that remains through which we can explain these reports?  This question draws attention to the basic shortcoming of the argument from apparitions.  At best, this argument--like others of the empirical sort--can only provide us with rational grounds for regarding the survival theory as probably true, but not as definitely established.

The Argument from Near-Death Experiences

Let us consider one further argument in support of the survival theory.  We may refer to it as the "argument from near-death experiences."  As the name indicates, this argument invokes what are called "near-death experiences" in support of the view that there is life after death.  Although this phenomenon has been widely reported, from the remote past up to modern times, the considerable attention which it has received in recent years is largely due to the publication of a book entitled *Life After Life*, by Dr. Raymond A. Moody, who received his Ph.D. in philosophy from the University of Virginia.  In order to clarify the nature of this phenomenon, I will quote selected passages from this work.

At the present time, I know of approximately 150 cases of this phenomenon.  The experiences which I have studied fall into three distinct categories:

(1) The experiences of persons who were resuscitated after having been thought, adjudged, or pronounced clinically dead by their doctors.

(2) The experiences of persons who, in the course of accidents or severe injury or illness, came very close to physical death.

(3) The experiences of persons who, as they died, told them to other

people who were present.  Later, these other people reported the content of the death experience to me.[8]

Noting definite similarities among the 150 cases which he studied, Dr. Moody proceeds to construct an "ideal" case of the near-death experience:

A man is dying and, as he reaches the point of greatest physical distress, he hears himself pronounced dead by his doctor.  He begins to hear an uncomfortable noise, a loud ringing or buzzing, and at the same time feels himself moving very rapidly through a long dark tunnel.  After this, he suddenly finds himself outside of his own physical body, but still in the immediate physical environment, and he sees his own body from a distance, as though he is a spectator. He watches the resuscitation attempt from this unusual vantage point and is in a state of emotional upheaval.
After a while, he collects himself and becomes more accustomed to his odd condition.  He notices that he still has a "body," but one of a very different nature and with very different powers from the physical body he has left behind.  Soon other things begin to happen.  Others come to meet and to help him.  He glimpses the spirits of relatives and friends who have already died, and a loving, warm spirit of a kind he has never encountered before--a being of light--appears before him.  This being asks him a question, nonverbally, to make him evaluate his life and helps him along by showing him a panoramic instantaneous playback of the major events of his life.  At some point he finds himself approaching some sort of barrier or border, apparently representing the limit between earthly life and the next life.  Yet, he finds that he must go back to the earth, that the time for his death has not yet come.  At this point he resists, for now he is taken up with his experiences in the afterlife and does not want to return.  He is overwhelmed by intense feelings of joy, love, and peace.  Despite his attitude, though, he somehow reunites with his physical body and lives.
Later he tries to tell others, but he has trouble doing so.  In the first place, he can find no human words adequate to describe these unearthly episodes.  He also finds that others scoff, so he stops telling other people.  Still, the experience affects his life profoundly, especially his views about death and its relationship to life.[9]

I wish to reiterate that countless cases similar to 150 studied by Dr.

Moody have been reported, from the earliest periods of history. For example, over 300 years before the birth of Christ, in Book X of the *Republic*, Plato recounts the story of a warrior by the name of Er, son of Armenius. Er is said to have been slain on the battlefield, and it is reported that, after his death, he found himself in another world. However, subsequently, having been shown many things of importance in the afterlife, Er revives, and resumes his life on the physical plane.

Another case that underscores the antiquity of such accounts, and which is among those mentioned by Moody, is reported by the Venerable Bede. In the year A.D. 731, he finished his work entitled *A History of the English Church and People*. In this book he relates the "noteworthy miracle" of a certain individual, who "already dead," returned "to bodily life," and told of "many notable things that he had seen."

> ...This was the account he used to give of his experience: "A handsome man in a shining robe was my guide, and we walked in silence in what appeared to be a northeasterly direction. As we traveled onward, we came to a very broad and deep valley of infinite length....He soon brought me out of darkness into an atmosphere of clear light, and as he led me forward in bright light, I saw before us a tremendous wall which seemed to be of infinite length and height in all directions. As I could see no gate, window, or entrance in it, I began to wonder why we went up to the wall. But when we reached it, all at once--I know not by what means--we were on top of it. Within lay a very broad and pleasant meadow....Such was the light flooding all this place that it seemed greater than the brightness of daylight or of the sun's rays at noon....
> "The guide said, 'You must now return to your body and live among men once more; but if you will weigh your actions with greater care and study to keep your words and ways virtuous and simple, then when you die you too will win a home among these happy spirits that you see.' .... When he told me this, I was most reluctant to return to my body; for I was entranced by the pleasantness and beauty of the place.... But I did not dare to question my guide, and meanwhile, I know not how, I suddenly found myself alive among men once more."[10]

Keeping these examples in mind, let us utilize the following simple formulation:

(1) Premise:   If there were no life after death, then near-death experiences would not occur.
(2) Premise:   But, near-death experiences DO occur.
CONCLUSION:   Therefore, there IS life after death.

The plausibility of this argument, like that of the foregoing, depends on the extent to which explanations other than survival can be ruled out. In other words, if the only way in which we can satisfactorily explain the innumerable reports of near-death experiences is by assuming that "dead" persons continue to live, in another world, then this argument is maximally persuasive. But, the difficulty here is precisely that of ruling out other explanations. For example, how can we be sure that these near-death experiences are not simply "terminal physiological processes," as has often been suggested? Could not these near-death experiences amount merely to a "winding down" of the brain's electro-chemical activity? This indeed is the very explanation which materialists have insisted on ever since the publication of Moody's first book on the subject.

Accordingly, our conclusion must be that the argument from near-death experiences, at best, can only justify the inference that the survival theory is probably correct, not decisively proven.

*Notes*

[1] Hackforth, R. (trans.), *Plato's Phaedo* (Cambridge: Cambridge University Press, 1972), pp. 81 and 84.
[2] Abdu'l-Baha, *The Promulgation of Universal Peace* (Wilmette: Baha'i Publishing Trust, 1982), 415.
[3] Hamilton, E., and Cairns, H. (eds.), *The Collected Dialogues of Plato* (Princeton: Princeton University Press, 1961), pp. 492-493.
[4] Abdu'l-Baha, *Some Answered Questions* (Wilmette: Baha'i Publishing Trust, 1981), pp. 239-240.
[5] Myers, F.W.H., *Human Personality and its Survival of Bodily Death* (London and New York: Longman, 1903), Vol. II: 27-30.
[6] Ducasse, C.J., *The Belief in a Life After Death* (Springfield: Charles C. Thomas Publisher, 1961), pp. 154-155.

[7]Ibid., p. 155.
[8]Moody, Raymond A., *Life After Life* (New York: Bantam Books, 1975), p. 16.
[9]Ibid., pp. 21-23.
[10]Bede, *A History of the English Church and People* (Harmondsworth, England:  Penguin Books, 1968), pp. 289-293.

CHAPTER SEVEN:


THE PROBLEM OF EVIL

## CHAPTER 7: The Problem of Evil

In previous chapters our thinking has centered on the concept of God, and that of spiritual beings. A significant part of what we did involved the consideration of arguments in favor of the existence of God and the survival of spiritual beings beyond physical death. In the remainder of this book, God and Spirit will continue to be the focus of our concern. However, we shall now turn to the task of examining certain arguments against the aforementioned beliefs. More specifically, the present chapter takes up the so-called problem of evil, as the basis of and argument against God's existence; chapter 8 deals with the thesis that mental life depends on brain-activity, as the basis of an argument against survival; and chapter 9 focuses on the direct realist theory of sense-perception as an important factor in irreligion.

### Statement of the Argument

The problem of evil is perhaps the most serious of all challenges to theistic belief. Speaking more directly, let us employ the expression "argument from evil" as a designation for the attempted disproof of God's existence based on the phenomenon of evil. The argument from evil is a very simple piece of reasoning. This attempt at proving that God does exist may be formulated as follows:

(1) Premise: If God existed, then there would be no evil whatsoever in the entire universe.
(2) Premise: But, there is in fact an abundance of evil in the universe.
CONCLUSION: Therefore, God does not exist.

## God and Evil as Incompatible

Let us consider in turn the two premises of this argument. According to the conditional statement set forth as premise (1), the existence of God would make it altogether impossible for there to be any such thing as evil. But what justification is there for the claim that if God exists, then evil does not? In other words, why would God's existence guarantee the non-existence of evil? In an effort to state the position which most proponents of the argument from evil take on this question, I shall first employ the very terms which they typically make use of; subsequently, an alternative way of wording the relevant points will be suggested, in order to clarify this position further.

The usual account begins by noting certain attributes which God supposedly possesses, namely the attributes of omniscience, omnipotence, and omni-benevolence. To say that God is omniscient amounts to saying that God KNOWS ALL; to say that God is omnipotent is to say that God has ALL POWER; and to say that God is omni-benevolent amounts to the claim that God is ALL-GOOD, i.e., has all GOOD-WILL. Now, if God exists, then it necessarily follows that a Being exists *who has all three* of these attributes. But if there is in existence a Being who not only knows all, but in addition is all-powerful and all-good, then this fact would necessitate the non-existence of evil. For, if there exists a Being who is all-knowing, this Being IS AWARE of the means by which evil may be kept from ever existing; moreover, if this Being is all-powerful, then this Being HAS THE POWER to keep evil from ever existing; and if this Being is all-good, then this Being HAS THE DESIRE to keep evil from ever existing. Now, if a Being exists who knows how evil might be kept from ever existing, and at the same time has both the power and the desire to apply this knowledge, then it necessarily follows that evil does not exist. This is the basic line of reasoning usually advanced by proponents of the argument from evil in support of premise (1) above.

## An Alternative Argument

However, I wish to offer an alternative formulation of these points using the terminology suggested earlier in our discussion of the concept of God. This alternative account--unlike the account given above--is not exclusively tied to an anthropomorphic view of God. In our previous analysis of the concept of God, we arrived at the following view: God is that Something or Someone that is superlatively causative. Now, to say that God is *superlatively* causative is to say that God (1) causes MOST EXTENSIVELY, AND (2) causes MOST EXCELLENTLY. Moreover, to cause most *extensively* is to be the cause of EVERYTHING. More explicitly put, that which causes most extensively is necessarily the cause not only of all BEINGS, but also of all CONDITIONS and OCCURRENCES. Furthermore, to cause most *excellently* is to cause the BEST CONCEIVABLE beings and the BEST CONCEIVABLE conditions and occurrences. Let us examine these two facets of superlative causation a bit more closely.

As noted, part of what we mean when we say that God is superlatively causative is that God is causative most extensively, which is to say that God is the cause of all BEINGS, CONDITIONS, and OCCURRENCES. Using more traditional language, we may say that God is the CREATOR, in order to stress that He is the cause of all BEINGS or ENTITIES; and we may refer to God as the one RULER, to emphasize that he is the cause of all CONDITIONS and OCCURRENCES. That is, to *create* is to be the cause of BEINGS, and to *rule* is to be the cause of the CONDITIONS and OCCURRENCES which beings sustain and go through. Let us now briefly examine some divergent views of divine creativity and rulership, in order to develop clear thoughts in this sphere.

## God's Creativity

We may being with a look at some of the different ways of understanding God's creativity. Specifically, there are three views of divine creativity which we shall consider. These views may be designated as follows: (1) The *Ex Nihilo* Theory of Creation, (2) The Transformationist Theory of Creation, and (3) The Emanationist Theory of Creation. Each of these views will be considered in turn.

The words "ex nihilo" are taken from Latin; they mean *from nothing*. According to the *ex nihilo* theory of creation, to say that God is the Creator of something, x, implies that he performed a certain act (or set of acts) *at a definite point in time*, and that prior to this time x was absolutely NOTHING (i.e., x was wholly NON-EXISTENT). In other words, on this view of creation, saying that God is the Creator of x amounts to the claim that before the creative act of God x was utterly non-existent, and that only afterwards, and by means of this creative act, did x go from non-existence to existence. Thus, x was NOTHING, but subsequently, through God's act, x BECAME something.

Now, anyone who makes a real effort to think into the implications of this conception will come up against what appears to be a logical absurdity. For, this view of creation requires us to believe that pure nothingness CAN BECOME. But, to say that pure nothingness can become implies that pure nothingness has the *capacity*, or power, to become; and if pure nothingness *has capacity or power*, then pure nothingness is NOT pure nothingness. Thus, we are led to a logical absurdity. Let us seek to acquire further clarity on this point by reflecting on the following statements of Abdu 'l-Baha:

> Moreover, absolute nonexistence cannot become existence. If the beings were absolutely nonexistent, existence would not have come into being ... If it be said that such a thing came into existence from nonexistence, this does not refer to absolute nonexistence, but means that its former condition in relation to its actual condition was nothingness. For absolute nothingness cannot find existence, as it has not the capacity of existence.[1]

In other words, pure nothingness has no capacities, or powers, whatsoever; and if pure nothingness has no capacities, or powers, at all, then pure nothingness does not have the capacity, or power, TO BECOME something. In short, the *ex nihilo* theory of creation is correct only if pure nothingness has the capacity to become something; but pure nothingness does not have this (or any other) capacity. Therefore, the *ex nihilo* view of creation is not correct.

The transformationist theory of creation is immune to the criticism levelled above against the *ex nihilo* view. How does the transformationist view avoid the logical absurdity which attaches to the *ex nihilo* theory?

According to the transformationist theory, there is a material, or stuff, upon which God acts, in his role as Creator; and this material, or stuff, is co-eternal with God. That is, being eternal *together with* God, this material is both beginningless and endless. It has always existed along with God in the past, and will continue always to exist along with God in the future. But, despite the co-eternity of this material with God, the transformationist theory maintains that God nevertheless retains his superior status as Creator. On this view, God's creativity consists in the fact that he imposes order upon what would otherwise remain in a state of utter chaos.

In the role of Creator, God is thought to work upon a pre-existing material, to establish harmonious conditions within it, and to bring about orderly configurations and arrangements among its elements. That is, without the creative action of God, all of the materials which now constitute the universe would have remained in a condition of disorder. Thus, for example, without God's creativity, the materials which now go into the make-up of the sun and planets would never have been formed into spheres, and this group of spheres would never have been formed into a solar system (i.e., with the sun placed neatly at the center and the planets revolving around this center in an orderly fashion). Briefly, according to the transformationist view, God's action of creating consists simply in the *transforming* of a pre-existent and disordered material into harmonious patterns.

But, there is a problem with this view of the divine creativity, namely this: By virtue of being superlatively causative, God is causative to the greatest conceivable extent, that is, divine causation must extend to ALL entities, events, and circumstances. Thus, to say that there is anything whose very existence is not wholly caused by God is implicitly to deny the existence of God; for, it implicitly denies that there is anything whose causativeness extends to everything. Or, alternatively, we could state the difficulty this way: To say that something exists whose existence is NOT caused by that which is the cause of ALL existence is self-contradictory. But, the transformationist view maintains that, apart from God, there exists a material, or stuff, of whose existence God is not the cause. For, on the transformationist view, God simply transforms this material, he does not cause its very existence. We see, therefore, that the transformationist view, while avoiding the particular absurdity of the *ex nihilo* position, nonetheless, encounters a logical difficulty of its own, and this difficulty is no less fatal than the former.

We turn now to the third view listed above, i.e., the emanationist theory of creation. The central idea of this view can be stated in terms of certain concepts we employed earlier for a different purpose. According to the emanationist theory, God causes the existence of beings co-temporally, not successionally. That is to say, all beings have a relation to God of absolute dependence, but this relation of dependence *never had a beginning* and will not end. Thus, on this view of creation, to speak of God's creativity is simply to underscore the fact that the existence of all beings is WHOLLY DETERMINED by God, and that this existencedetermination has neither commencement nor termination. Or, alternatively, we could state the point this way: According to the emanationist view, all entities exist BY MEANS of God, but this existing-by-means-of-God did not start at some particular point in the past; rather, the creatures have always existed, and God has always been the cause of their existence.

In surveying the history of philosophy, one discovers that from very ancient times many have recognized this as one possible way of understanding creation. The description "emanationist" stems from the fact that this view can be defined in terms of an analogy, namely this one: Creatures emanate from God as light emanates from the sun. However, it should be borne in mind that the emanation of light from the sun is a relevant comparison only insofar as this light is thought of as having a *beginningless-endless* relationship of dependence to the sun, and not as coming *into existence* by means of it.

Now, the following logical absurdities led to the rejection of the first two views of creation: (1) Utter nothingness IS ABLE to become something; and (2) God exists together with something whose existence does not depend on God. The *ex nihilo* view avoids absurdity (2), but is untenable by reason of absurdity (1). The transformationist view avoids absurdity (1), but is untenable due to absurdity (2). But the emanationist view of creation avoids both of these absurdities. Consequently, when reference is made henceforth to God's creativity, it is the emanationist view which is intended.

## God's Rulership

Having looked at some divergent views of divine creativity, let us now turn our attention to some differing conceptions that relate to divine rulership. Since God must be conceived of as *superlatively* causative, it follows that God is to be thought of as causative to the greatest conceivable extent; hence, the concept of God is the concept of a Something or Someone that is the cause of all beings, and of all conditions and occurrences. To speak of God as the one Ruler is to underscore God's causativeness in connection with the latter; that is, to say that God is the one Ruler amounts to the claim that God is the cause of all CONDITIONS and OCCURRENCES.

But divine rulership, conceived of in this manner, immediately gives rise to a certain problem. That problem is the following: There at least seems to be such a thing as free action on the part of human beings; so, if this is indeed the case, then how can there be any such thing as absolute rulership on the part of God? For, to say that human actions are free implies that human beings are the causes of their own actions, and to say that God's rulership over things is absolute implies that God is the cause of ALL occurrences, even including human actions. Let us consider in turn three relevant positions. We may adopt the following names to designate these differing views: (1) Fatalism, (2) Libertarianism, and (3) Compatibilism.

Fatalism is the view that in reality there is no such thing as free action on the part of human beings, since all occurrences (including human actions) are caused by God. This view presupposes that the causation-of-all-occurrences-by-God would make it impossible for there to be any occurrences caused by human beings. In other words, if God is the cause of *all* occurrences, then humans cannot cause any occurrences (not even human actions).

In opposition to fatalism, libertarianism maintains the following: There is no such thing as absolute rulership on the part of God, since at least some occurrences (namely, human actions) are caused by human beings. The presupposition here is that the causation-of-some-occurrences-by-humans implies that God is not the cause of all occurrences. That is, if humans cause *some* occurrences, then God cannot be the cause of *all* occurrences.

Now, fatalism and libertarianism have in common the assumption that absolute rulership in God and free action in humans are mutually exclusive, i.e., that it is impossible to have both. But, it is precisely this assumption which compatibilism rejects. According to the compatibilist view, God's rulership over things is absolute, and at the same time, human actions are free. Thus, compatibilism maintains that God is the cause of all occurrences, but that human beings, nevertheless, cause their own actions. This obviously presupposes that the causation-of-all-occurrences-by-God does not imply that humans do not cause their own actions. Moreover, it is clear that, on this view, the causation-of-some-occurrences-by-humans does not imply that God is not the cause of all occurrences. Briefly, this view regards absolute rulership and free action as mutually compatible.

Now, in examining these three views, one easily sees the particular difficulty which each involves. In rejecting free action, fatalism denies what seems to be an obvious fact of human experience. On the other hand, libertarianism is wedded to the logically untenable position that God exists, and nevertheless is not the cause of all occurrences; this position is untenable on purely logical grounds, for it amounts to the claim that something exists which *is* the cause of all occurrences, but nevertheless, *is not* the cause of all occurrences. As for compatibilism, this view strikes many as nothing less than a complete paradox. For, how could it be that the very actions which humans *freely* perform are at the same time actions *ordained* by God?

The first thing to note is that the term "free" is not equivalent to "uncaused." For, if these terms were strictly equivalent, then compatibilism would indeed be hopelessly paradoxical. But, to say that human actions are free does not imply that they are uncaused; on the contrary, free actions are necessarily caused actions. More specifically, a free action is an action which is caused BY THE VERY PERSON WHO PERFORMS IT. Thus, an action which has no cause cannot be a free action.

But, even though describing an action as "free" implies that it is caused by the person who performs it, it should also be noted that to call an action "free" does not necessarily imply that the person who performs it is its original (or "first") cause. It is conceivable that a certain action could be caused by the person who performs it, and hence free, while at the same time having an ORIGINAL cause other than the person who performs it. Let us consider this point more carefully.

Prior to the performance of every free act, the doer of that act is already DISPOSED to perform that act freely. That is, the doer of any given free act must already possess the specific DISPOSITION of which that act is the expression, even before that act is performed. Now, the original cause of any given disposition is also the original cause of the action which arises from that disposition. But God, as Creator, must be regarded as the original cause of all the dispositions which underlie free action. Therefore, God must also be the *original* cause of all free action. In other words, God's absolute rulership in connection with free action is an inescapable consequence of the divine creativity.

This matter may also be looked at from another point of view. The actual performance of any given free action depends on the existence of suitable circumstances, i.e., circumstances which permit that free act to be performed. For example, the specific set of actions which constitute swimming are free actions insofar as a swimmer causes these actions himself, or herself. Nevertheless, in order for one actually to swim, circumstances must be such that one has access to a body of water. Access to a body of water is among the requirements on which the actual performance of these free actions depends. Similar considerations apply to the case of every free action; that is, the actual performance of free actions invariably depends on the existence of a suitable context. Therefore, since God, as Ruler, is the cause of the circumstances on which the performance of every free action depends, it follows that God is also the cause of the actual performance of free actions.

To clarify this point further, I wish to employ an example which occurs in the correspondence of the French philosopher Rene Descartes. In a letter written to Princess Elizabeth of Bohemia, Descartes makes use of an analogy. He asks the princess to imagine two men who have a nature, or disposition, such that if they were ever brought together, then they would FREELY choose to fight each other. Now, it is in the power of the king to determine whether or not they come together. He may either bring the two men together, or keep them apart; moreover, the king is fully aware of the men's dispositions, and thus, of the results associated with their coming together and staying apart.

I wish to raise the following question about Descartes' example: Is it not accurate to say that if the men fight, then the king is the cause of their fighting, and also, that if they do not fight, then the king is the cause of their not fighting? If so, then parallel considerations should be applicable to the case of God and human beings *vis-a-vis* free action. That is, just as the king would be the cause of the fighting in which the two men *freely* engaged, so God must be thought of as the cause of what human beings freely do; for, God must be conceived of as controlling the circumstances on which the performance of free actions depends.

The purpose of these remarks has been to dispel the appearance of paradox that characterizes the compatibilist position. Therefore, on the assumption that this has in some measure been achieved, I shall adopt compatibilism in the ensuing discussion, as being the most plausible of the three views of divine rulership listed.

We have been examining one aspect of the notion of superlative causation, namely the EXTENT of such causation. But, to say that God is superlatively causative is not only to assert that he is most extensively causative, it also implies that God is most EXCELLENTLY causative. Let us briefly review the relevant points pertaining to this second aspect of the concept of superlative causation. To say that God is most excellently causative implies that God causes the BEST CONCEIVABLE beings, and the BEST CONCEIVABLE conditions and occurrences. Now, when we consider conjointly the implications of these two facets of the concept of superlative causation, it becomes altogether clear that premise (1) of the argument from evil is justified. That is this premise asserts that the existence of God would guarantee the non-existence of evil, and this very assertion is a logical consequence derivable from the notion of superlative causation. For, since God must be conceived of both as most extensively causative and as most excellently causative, it follows that God must be thought of both as the cause of ALL beings, conditions, and occurrences, and as causing the BEST CONCEIVABLE beings, conditions, and occurrences.

Moreover, it should be kept in mind that adoption of an emanationist-compatibilist position allows us to say in the very strictest sense that the divine causation is maximal. That is, the emanationist view of creation implies that the existence and nature of beings are WHOLLY determined by God; and the compatibilist view of rulership implies that God's control extends to all conditions and occurrences without ANY EXCEPTIONS whatsoever. From what has been said it follows that if God really does exist, then all beings that exist and all conditions and occurrences that come about are the BEST CONCEIVABLE. That is, the existence of God would guarantee the best conceivable beings, conditions, and occurrences. But, the best conceivable beings, conditions, and occurrences are entirely NON-EVIL. In other words, if God exists, then everything is good, and if everything is good, then nothing is evil. From this it clearly follows that the existence of God would guarantee the non-existence of evil, which is to say that premise (1) of the argument from evil is true.

## The Existence of Evil

But what about the second premise of the argument from evil? Premise (2) in the above formulation claims that evil does exist. What justification is there for this claim? Those who rely on the argument from evil in order to disprove God's existence point to two main categories of phenomena to support the assertion that evil exists. On the one hand, they call attention to such things as hatred, cruelty, greed, selfishness, malice, envy, deceit, murder, oppression, and genocide; such things are called forms of wickedness, i.e., *moral* evil. On the other hand, they point to such things as disease, decrepitude, poverty, earthquakes, tornadoes, hurricanes (and other natural disasters), auto accidents, fires, plane crashes, and to all of the pain, suffering, destruction, and death which are associated with such occurrences; these are called misfortunes, or varieties of *physical* evil. Thus, the rational justification which is offered for premise (2) is this: Numerous instances of wickedness and misfortune clearly do exist, and since all of these instances of wickedness and misfortune are varieties of EVIL, it follows that evil exists.

We see then that in providing rational support for the claim that evil exists, proponents of the argument from evil have recourse to the assertion that the various things enumerated under the categories of wickedness and misfortune are in fact evil. To facilitate statement of the point I wish to make here, let us understand the words " wickedness" and "misfortune" as non-descriptive labels, as neutral "tags," so to speak. In this way we can employ these words simply as a means by which to call attention to the two categories of things mentioned above, without any pre-judgment as to whether or not these things are evil. Let us put the main point here more concisely as follows: In trying to establish that evil exists, proponents of the argument from evil rely on the assertion that wickedness and misfortune are evil.

Now the claim that wickedness and misfortune are evil is simply taken for granted by the typical proponent of this argument. That wickedness and misfortune are evil is assumed to be so OBVIOUS a fact as not to require any proof. But is such an assumption really justified? Are wickedness and misfortune so obviously evil that it is not necessary to establish the point through rational means? I shall state and defend an answer to this question in what follows.

First of all, in the interest of clarity, we need a definite criterion for deciding whether something is evil. Let us adopt the following criterion: Any given condition or occurrence is EVIL if and only if that condition or occurrence is such that a fully rational being, in taking adequate awareness of it, would find it to be a source of displeasure, i.e., would disapprove of it. With this criterion, the important question to ask is whether or not a given condition or occurrence would be approvingly contemplated by a RATIONAL being, not whether such a condition or occurrence would involve painful sensations for a SENTIENT being.

A *rational* being is a being that has the ability to THINK, and thus, to arrive at an appraisal of things through UNDERSTANDING them. It should be stressed, moreover, that the word "adequate" requires that the mentioned awareness should extend beyond the isolated condition, or occurrence, as such; that is, the word "adequate" is used, in order to underscore that this awareness must extend to the point of encompassing past, contemporaneous, and future conditions (and occurrences) which are relevant to the appraisal of the condition (or occurrence) in question.

In order to clarify the concept of evil which use of this criterion presupposes, I quote from the writings of Baha'u' llah. In his short work entitled *The Seven Valleys*, Baha'u' llah utilizes richly figurative language in order to set forth various abstruse points touching on spiritual philosophy and mysticism:

> There was once a lover who had sighed for long years in separation from his beloved, and wasted in the fire of remoteness. From the rule of love, his heart was empty of patience, and his body weary of his spirit; he reckoned life without her as a mockery, and time consumed him away. How many a day he found no rest in longing for her; how many a night the pain of her kept him from sleep; his body was worn to a sigh, his heart's wound had turned him to a cry of sorrow. He had given a thousand lives for one taste of the cup of her presence, but it availed him not. The doctors knew no cure for him, and companions avoided his company; yea, physicians have no medicine for one sick of love, unless the favor of the beloved one deliver him.

At last, the tree of his longing yielded the fruit of despair, and the fire of his hope fell to ashes. Then one night he could live no more, and he went out of his house and made for the market-place. On a sudden, a watchman followed after him. He broke into a run, with the watchman following; then other watchmen came together, and barred every passage to the weary one. And the wretched one cried from his heart, and ran here and there, and moaned to himself: "Surely this watchman is Izra'il, my angel of death, following so fast upon me; or he is a tyrant of men, seeking to harm me." His feet carried him on, the one bleeding with the arrow of love, and his heart lamented. Then he came to a garden wall, and with untold pain he scaled it, for it proved very high; and forgetting his life, he threw himself down to the garden.

And there he beheld his beloved with a lamp in her hand, searching for a ring she had lost. When the heart-surrendered lover looked on his ravishing love, he drew a great breath and raised up his hands in prayer, crying: "O God! Give Thou glory to the watchman, and riches and long life. For the watchman was Gabriel, guiding this poor one; or he was Israfil, bringing life to this wretched one!"[2]

This passage contains an abundance of symbolism, but it will suffice for present purposes to note that the watchman stands for all conditions and occurrences of an ostensibly negative character which are encountered in life; he represents the various forms of WICKEDNESS and MISFORTUNE which every human being must in some measure meet with in life. The lover, of course, represents the individual human being who must experience life's ordeals and vicissitudes. But, what it is most important for us to notice here is that the "lover's" praise for the watchman comes at the end of this passage, when he has gained an ADEQUATE AWARENESS of his experiences with the watchman, and is thus able to view them in the light of other occurrences of relevance to their appraisal.

Referring to the lover's words of praise concerning the watchman, Baha'u'llah continues as follows:

Indeed, his words were true, for he had found many a secret justice in this seeming tyranny of the watchman, and seen how many a mercy lay hid behind the veil. Out of wrath, the guard had led him who was athirst in love's desert to the sea of his loved one, and lit up the dark night of absence with light of reunion. He had driven one who was afar, into the garden of nearness, had guided an ailing soul to the heart's physician.

Now if the lover could have looked ahead, he would have blessed the watchman at the start, and prayed on his behalf, and he would have seen that tyranny as justice; but since the end was veiled to him, he moaned and made his plaint in the beginning. Yet those who journey in the garden-land of knowledge, because they see the end in the beginning, see peace in war and friendliness in anger.[3]

Again, the metaphorical content of this quotation is considerable. However, what is especially germane is Baha'u'llah's statement that "if the lover could have looked ahead, he would have blessed the watchman at the start ..., and would have seen that tyranny as justice ..." Though the lover complained in the beginning, nonetheless, once he had acquired an *adequate awareness* of what he had gone through, he, as a rational being, could no longer disapprove of it.

The philosopher Leibniz used to try to convey these same points through the use of a different metaphor, namely that of an extremely beautiful painting. Consistently with this Leibnizian analogy, the totality of conditions and occurrences (i.e., all past, present, and future conditions and occurrences) may be compared to a painting of surpassing beauty. But, if we imagine this painting to be entirely covered, except for a very small portion of it, then the small part of the painting which can be seen might be characterized by ugliness or discord. But if the hole in the covering is made larger, so that larger sections of the painting are exposed, then the ugliness or discord which seemed to characterize the one portion of it will vanish. Leibniz's point, of course, is that every instance of wickedness or misfortune which we encounter in life is like the small portion of this painting that is exposed to view. In other words, if a fully rational being were to gain an adequate awareness of this wickedness and misfortune, then he would cease to disapprove of them; and it is just the lack of such adequate awareness which gives rise to the *consciousness* of evil.

Let us return now to the question we raised earlier. We had taken note of the fact that proponents of the argument from evil rely on the following argument: Numerous instances of wickedness and misfortune clearly do exist, and since all of these instances of wickedness and misfortune are varieties of EVIL, it follows that evil does exist. Then we raised a question about this argument, namely this: Are the various instances of wickedness and misfortune so obviously evil that there is no need to provide rational support for this claim? That is, may it simply be taken for granted that wickedness and misfortune are evil? Using the criterion of evil set forth previously, we may now answer this question as follows. It is JUST OBVIOUS that the various instances of wickedness and misfortune are evil only if it is JUST OBVIOUS that each of these instances of wickedness and misfortune is such that a fully rational being who took adequate awareness of it would find it to be a source of displeasure, i.e., would disapprove of it. But it is NOT just obvious that each of these instances of wickedness and misfortune would be disapproved of by a fully rational being who took adequate awareness of it. Consequently, it is NOT just obvious that the various instances of wickedness and misfortune are evil. Thus, insofar as proponents of the argument from evil suppose it to be just obvious that wickedness and misfortune are evil, they are mistaken.

Moreover, if any degree of doubt attaches to the contention that wickedness and misfortune are evil, then this same degree of doubt also attaches to premise (2) of the argument from evil. For, premise (2) claims that evil does exist, and the reasoning on which this claim is based (namely, "Wickedness and misfortune exist, *and are evil*, so evil exists") contains that contention as a key premise. In other words, the only reason which proponents of the argument from evil offer to back up their claim that evil exists is that such things as cruelty, hate, pain, sickness, and death exist; therefore, insofar as it can be shown that things like cruelty, pain, etc., are not just obviously evil, their claim that evil exists can be doubted, and, consequently, the argument from evil, in which this claim appears as a premise, is lacking in persuasive force. Furthermore, it was for this very purpose (i.e., in order to show that wickedness and misfortune are not just obviously evil) that I proposed above a definite criterion of evil, and invited reflection on certain analogies employed by Baha'u'llah and the philosopher Leibniz.

Nevertheless, to suggest that wickedness and misfortune are perhaps not evil is counter-intuitive. For, each human being inevitably either personally experiences, or at least becomes informed about, a host of ostensible negatives during the course of life, and it seems altogether false to maintain that such negatives (such brutality, oppression, pain, disease, destruction, and so on) are anything other than pure evil. The counter-intuitive character of this suggestion poses a difficulty for any believer-in-God whose rejection of the argument from evil is based on a denial of premise (2).

However, this difficulty vanishes when we recognize that our disinclination to admit that wickedness and misfortune are perhaps not evil assumes a different sense of the word "evil" from the one which is assumed by the criterion of evil I set forth above. Let me try to state this a bit more clearly.

Consider the following, less stringent, criterion for deciding whether something is evil: Any given condition or occurrence is evil if and only if that condition or occurrence is such that a fully rational being, in taking awareness of it, would find it to be a source of displeasure, i.e., would disapprove of it. What distinguishes this criterion from the one previously proposed is simply the omission of the word "adequate". That is, in this case there is no requirement that the mentioned rational awareness should extend beyond the isolated condition or occurrence as such; it does not have to encompass any of the past, contemporaneous, or future conditions and occurrences that are bound up with the one to be assessed.

Now, if we use this less stringent criterion, what must we conclude with respect to the merits of the argument from evil? On this criterion, it is clear that premise (2) would have to be regarded as true. For, the various forms of wickedness and misfortune doubtless do exist, and each instance of such wickedness and misfortune--when considered *in isolation* from other conditions and occurrences--would be found by a fully rational being to be a source of displeasure. Thus, if such disapproval on the part of a fully rational being is a sufficient condition for us to be justified in regarding something as evil, then we may conclude that each instance of wickedness or misfortune IS EVIL. From this it would follow that evil does exist, which is to say that premise (2) is true.

Accordingly, the less stringent criterion forces us to say that evil exists. But, what about premise (1) of the argument from evil? Recall that, according to premise (1), the existence of God would guarantee the non-existence of evil, or in other words, God's existence is not compatible with the existence of evil. Does adoption of the less stringent criterion of evil in any way impact upon the plausibility of this premise? As a matter of fact, if we adopt this criterion, then we must conclude that premise (1) of the argument from evil IS FALSE. That is, if we take "evil" in the sense of this second criterion, then it is logically permissible to say that both God and evil exist.

The final outcome of our reflections, therefore, is this: If we understand "evil" in the sense of the first, more stringent criterion, then premise (1) is true, but premise (2) is false (that is, if this kind of evil existed, then this would be sufficient proof that God does not exist, but in fact there is no such thing as evil, in this sense); hence, on that basis the argument from evil may be rejected. If, on the other hand, we understand "evil" in the sense of the second, and less stringent, criterion, then premise (2) is true, but premise (1) is false (that is, in this sense of the word, evil definitely does exist, but the existence of this kind of evil is compatible with the existence of God); and thus, the argument from evil may still be rejected. Consequently, it is possible to maintain a reasonable belief in the existence of God, even despite the formidable challenge posed by the argument from evil.

*Notes*

[1] Abdu 'l-Baha, *Some Answered Questions* (Wilmette: Baha'i Publishing Trust, 1918, pp. 180 & 281.
[2] Baha'u'llah, *The Seven Valleys and The Four Valleys* (Wilmette: Baha'i Publishing Trust, 1975), pp. 13-14.
[3] Ibid., pp. 14-15.

CHAPTER EIGHT:


THE BRAIN-DEPENDENCY
ARGUMENT

CHAPTER 8: The Brain-Dependency Argument

The main issue to be dealt with in this chapter is brought out clearly in the following pronouncements of the British philosopher Bertrand Russell (A.D. 1872-1970):

> What we call our "thoughts" seem to depend upon the organization of tracks in the brain in the same sort of way in which journeys depend upon roads and railways ... Mental phenomena seem to be bound up with material structure ... We cannot suppose that an individual's thinking survives bodily death, since that destroys the organization of the brain and dissipates the energy which utilized the brain tracks ... I believe that when I die I shall rot, and nothing of my ego will survive.[1]

The majority of thoughtful persons who reject the belief in life after death do so based on reasoning similar to that set forth by Russell in the above-quoted passage. I call this line of reasoning the "brain-dependency argument" against survival. The brain-dependency argument is probably the most powerful of the arguments which have been adduced in opposition to the idea of an afterlife. Hence, the central focus of our concern in this chapter will be with this particular argument against survival. The course which we shall follow may appear somewhat tortuous. However, everything brought out here will have relevance--either directly or indirectly--to our final assessment of the merits of this argument.

Let us again use the word "consciousness" to cover all varieties of awareness. On this usage, all mental phenomena are just so many different *modes* of consciousness. The brain-dependency argument, then, may be stated simply as follows:

> (1) Premise: If consciousness depends on brain- processes, then there can be no life after death. (2) Premise: As a matter of fact, consciousness does depend on brain-processes. CONCLUSION: Therefore, there can be no life after death.

The first premise of the argument is uncontroversial. That is, there can be no doubt but that such dependency would entail the impossibility of an afterlife. For if consciousness depends on brain-processes, then there can be no consciousness when brain-processes have ceased. Moreover, if consciousness depends on brain-processes, then a FINAL cessation of brain-processes (i.e., a cessation of brain-processes never to be followed by their return) must involve a FINAL cessation of consciousness (i.e., a cessation of consciousness never to be followed by the re-gaining of consciousness). Now, death undoubtedly involves a final cessation of brain-processes. Therefore, if consciousness depends on brain-processes, then death must involve a final cessation of consciousness. But, a *final* cessation of consciousness, i.e., a loss of consciousness which will never be followed by a re-gaining of consciousness, amounts to a *final* cessation of LIFE; for, if consciousness has been lost, and is never to be re-gained, then one cannot in the requisite sense say that life is present. To be sure, we could reasonably speak of someone's being *alive*, despite being perpetually unconscious. However, life in the sense intended by the expression "life after death" implies consciousness . From these considerations it clearly follows that if consciousness depends on brain-processes, then there can be no life after death, that is, premise ( 1 ) is true.

Let us now look at premise ( 2 ) of the brain-dependency argument. The second premise says this: Consciousness does in fact depend on brain-processes. But there are at least two different ways in which we can understand this assertion. On the one hand, the words "depends on" may be taken to mean *is caused exclusively by*; whereas, on the other hand, these words could be construed to mean *is identical with*. We shall examine these two interpretations in turn, and we shall seek to ascertain to what extent premise (2) is plausible on each interpretation.

To begin with, let us suppose that "depends on" means is caused exclusively by. According to this, when it is said that consciousness depends on brain-processes, this amounts to saying that consciousness is caused exclusively by brain-processes. Those who subscribe to the brain-dependency thesis in this sense of "depends on" typically assume as their basic metaphysical position some form of either (a) emergent materialism, or (b) epiphenomenalism. Let us see, in turn, what these two metaphysical positions essentially amount to, that is, insofar as they are pertinent to our discussion.

The relevant part of what emergent materialism maintains is this: If by "brain activity" we understand, in the last analysis, certain purely mechanical operations, that is, if brain activity as such is nothing but the *movement* of the material particles that make up the brain, in ever-shifting patterns, then consciousness is NOT strictly the same thing as brain activity. In other words, on this view, although consciousness is not merely the microscopic movement of brain-matter, it nonetheless does arise *on the basis of* such movement. Mental states such as joy, fear, visualizing, doubting, judging, understanding, etc., are not simply differing patterns of motion of the brain's material components; but, they do EMERGE (i.e., come into existence) as a result of such material motion. Moreover, it should be emphasized that, according to emergent materialism, there does not exist some other kind of reality, or substance, apart from matter. Thus, the consciousness which arises by means of the afore-mentioned brain-activity is not believed to be causally induced upon some spiritual substance distinct from the brain. Mental events such as thoughts, joy, fear, and so on, are not states of some non-material substance, rather they are believed to be certain special states of the material brain itself. For the emergent materialist, all is matter; hence, the brain is a purely material entity. Nevertheless, as a result of certain complex motions of its sub-atomic components, consciousness is said to be superadded to these purely material motions, and thereby the brain itself supposedly *becomes conscious.* Therefore, according to emergent materialism, it is the brain itself which thinks, understands, rejoices, fears, visualizes, pays attention, dreams, and so on. There is no need, on this view, to suppose the existence of a non-material soul, in order to explain these various mental states.

The second interpretation of the expression "depends on" is associated with a form of mind-body dualism called "epiphenomenalism". The central thesis of epiphenomenalism is that consciousness is an "epiphenomenon" (i.e., a by-product) of brain-activity. However, it is important to note that, as a form of dualism, epiphenomenalism affirms the existence of the soul or ego, as something distinct , i . e ., as a thing standing apart from the body . Thus, on this view, the soul is not the same thing as the brain, nor is the soul identical with any portion of the brain; rather, the soul is entirely OTHER THAN the brain. For epiphenomenalism, the body and soul are two different things; nevertheless, epiphenomenalism is to be distinguished from other forms of dualism, in that it regards the soul, or ego, as WHOLLY PASSIVE in its mental life. That is, the soul is regarded as wholly passive in the specific sense that it only passively *receives*, consciousness, through being "acted on" from outside itself. In other words, according to epiphenomenalism, the soul, if left to itself, would remain forever in a state of unconsciousness; and only by virtue of being connected to a rightly-functioning brain is the soul able to *become conscious* and *be maintained* in a state of consciousness.

It should be stressed that, on this view, the brain itself is NOT conscious. In other words, brain-processes as such are not mental phenomena; they are purely material processes. However, it is believed that the brain--through its processes--causes consciousness to arise as a phenomenon *in the soul* (or ego). In short, according to this view, to say that consciousness depends on brain-processes is simply to say that consciousness is a phenomenon which may arise in the soul, and that the actual rise of consciousness in the soul is caused exclusively by brain-processes. It is clear, then, that emergent materialism and epiphenomenalism have in common the supposition that consciousness depends on brain processes; but, they understands this dependency in slightly different ways.

Now, let us recall that premise (2) says: Consciousness does depend on brain-processes. When we take "depends on" in the sense common to emergent materialism and epiphenomenalism, to what extent can premise (2) be regarded as a plausible assertion? Or, we could put the question in this way: What rational justification is there for the claim that consciousness depends on brain-processes, if we take "depends on" as meaning *is caused exclusively by*?

To support their contention that consciousness depends on brain-processes, proponents of the brain-dependency argument usually call attention to the various ways in which people can be made to lose consciousness. They point out, for instance, that a forceful blow to the head can result in unconsciousness, or that a person can be made to lose consciousness through the administration of certain "psycho-active" drugs, as in general anesthesia for surgery. Let us use the case of a hard blow to the head, keeping in mind that what will be said with regard to this case is equally applicable to any of the other means of producing unconsciousness.

The first thing to consider is this: Premise (2), i.e., the statement "consciousness depends on brain-processes" is just one possible way of EXPLAINING the observed sequence of events. It is merely an ASSUMPTION which proponents of this argument make, in order to account for the fact that a heavy blow to the head is followed by unconsciousness. They do not actually observe such dependence, but rather they observe a certain *sequence*, and simply ASSUME such dependence. More specifically, proponents of the argument observe that a heavy blow to the head is invariably followed by what is ostensibly a state of unconsciousness. This gives us a two-element sequence:

blow-to-the-head > unconsciousness

But a third element is imaginatively introduced, namely a cessation of certain brain-processes. That is, a blow to the head supposedly causes certain brain-processes to cease, so that we come to have the three-element sequence:

blow-to-the-head > cessation of brain-processes >
loss of consciousness

Now, since the supposed cessation of certain brain-processes is followed by a loss of consciousness it is *inferred* that consciousness must DEPEND ON such brain-processes. In other words, the idea is that since consciousness stops, as soon as certain brain-processes stop, consciousness must be caused exclusively by brain-processes.

But the point I wish to emphasize is this: There are OTHER ways of explaining the observed sequence, apart from this assumption that consciousness depends on brain-processes. That is, even if the disruption of certain brain-processes is invariably followed by unconsciousness, this fact does not constitute PROOF that consciousness actually depends on brain-processes.

In order to clarify this point, I wish to call attention again to certain passages from the writings of Baha'u'llah. In these passages, Baha'u'llah not only gives a clear and fair statement of what is essentially the brain-dependency argument, he also provides an impressive refutation of this argument. In an admirably lucid, and decisive manner, Baha'u'llah shows in these passages that the brain-dependency argument against survival -- despite its *prima facie* plausibility --does not succeed. We may begin with the passage in which Baha'u'llah, in reply to questions raised by one of his followers, presents this argument, in order subsequently to refute it:

> Thou hast asked Me whether man, as apart from the Prophets of God and His chosen ones, will retain, after his physical death, the self-same individuality, personality, consciousness, and understanding that characterize his life in this world. If this should be the case, how is it, thou hast observed, that whereas such slight injuries to his mental faculties as fainting and severe illness deprive him of his understanding and consciousness, his death, which must involve the decomposition of his body and the dissolution of its elements, is powerless to destroy that understanding and extinguish that consciousness? How can any one imagine that man's consciousness and personality will be maintained, when the very instruments necessary to their existence and function will be completely disintegrated?[2]

Although the word "brain" is not used in the above quotation, nonetheless, it is clear that the reasoning set forth in this passage is precisely what we have called the "brain-dependency argument." After presenting the argument, Baha'u'llah proceeds to offer a powerful refutation of it. In order fully to appreciate the logical force of this Baha'i refutation of the brain-dependency argument, one should attentively read, and re-read, the following passage, making a real effort to penetrate through to its inner meaning:

> Know thou that the soul of man is exalted above, and is independent of all infirmities of body or mind. That a sick person showeth signs of weakness is due to the *hindrances that interpose themselves between his soul and his body,* for the soul itself remaineth itself remaineth unaffected by any bodily ailments. Consider the light of the lamp. Though an external object may interfere with its radiance,

the light itself continueth to shine with undiminished power. In like manner, every malady afflicting the body of man is *an impediment that preventeth the soul from manifesting its inherent might and power*. when It leaveth the body, however, it will evince such ascendancy, and reveal such influence as no force on earth can equal. Every pure, every refined and sanctified soul will be endowed with tremendous power, and shall rejoice with exceeding gladness.[3]

I would like to underscore two important points extractable from the above quotation. Firstly, according to the view there advanced, the soul (i.e., the ego or "I"), in and of itself, is NATURALLY conscious. That is, if the soul were left entirely to itself, free from all external influences, it would, so to speak, "shine" with the light of consciousness through an essential requirement of its own nature. To state the point metaphorically, the soul, on this view, is a SELF-LUMINOUS entity (like the sun as contrasted with the moon). But, the second point is this: Certain conditions and occurrences in the body are able temporarily to SUPPRESS the soul's consciousness. This view suggests that certain kinds of brain-processes may BLOCK the expression of consciousness in the soul, ie., may PREVENT the soul from *showing forth* in expression that consciousness which it is, in itself, INHERENTLY DISPOSED to show forth.

So then, according to this view, what happens when someone becomes unconscious following a heavy blow to the head, or after administration of a general anesthetic?

When someone suffers a heavy blow to the head, this may be assumed to INDUCE certain brain-processes, of an INHIBITORY character. That is, it may be supposed that the brain-state resulting from a heavy blow to the head temporarily blocks the natural action of the soul, temporarily hinders the soul from expressing itself as a conscious entity. Similarly, when unconsciousness is induced in a person through the administration of some psycho-active drug, it may be assumed that the action of the drug in that person's body merely brings about a certain brain-state which temporarily suppresses the soul's consciousness.

Thus, we see that the assumption that consciousness depends on brain processes, that, in other words, it cannot exist without brain-processes, is only ONE possible way of explaining the observed fact that events which presumably disrupt brain function (e.g., blows-to-the-head, drugs, etc.) are followed by a loss of consciousness. More specifically, it is equally possible to explain the observed sequence on the alternative assumption that the brain has a SUPPRESSIVE function, in addition to any consciousness-INDUCING function which it might possess.

In view of what has been said, it is clear that, however impressive it may seem at first glance, the brain-dependency argument does NOT constitute a definitive proof against life after death. Indeed, if the brain does suppress consciousness, while the soul in itself is inherently disposed to show forth consciousness, then the complete cessation of brain-activity which occurs at death -- far from being the cause of a loss of consciousness -- should actually result in an intensification or strengthening of consciousness.

So far, we have been considering an interpretation of "depends on" which is associated with emergent materialism and epiphenomenalism. But, what if we were to adopt a more purely materialistic interpretation of the words "depends on"? That is, what if we construe "depends on", in premise (2), as meaning *is identical with*? In that case, to say that consciousness depends on brain-processes implies that mental phenomena such as imagining, thinking, wishing, and so forth, are nothing but brain-processes. In other words, mental phenomena, on this view, are not merely caused exclusively by certain brain-processes; rather, they just are these brain-processes. This is a view which materialistic philosophers, from the most ancient times down to the present, have held to with the utmost confidence. Thus, in surveying the history of philosophy, we find that this is essentially the position taken by Charvaka of ancient India, the Roman poet Lucretius, the British philosopher Thomas Hobbes, the French thinker Julien de La Mettrie, the philosophers of Marxism, the recent philosopher Bertrand Russell, and by a large number of
present-day philosophers in many different countries. But, notwithstanding the great tenacity with which materialist philosophers have held to this position throughout history, it is, nonetheless, easily refuted. For, if we conceive of brain-processes in a strictly materialistic fashion, then the claim that consciousness is nothing but brain-activity is untenable on purely conceptual grounds.

Many philosophers have pointed this out, and indeed have shown definitively that no mental phenomenon can possibly be one-and-the-same-thing as a brain process, i.e., that consciousness is invariably something altogether distinct from brain-activity. This is sometimes called the "property objection" against materialism. One of the clearest statements of the so-called "property objection" is found in the *Monadology* of Leibniz:

> It must be confessed, however, that Perception, and that which depends upon it, are inexplicable by mechanical causes, that is to say, by figures and motions. Supposing that there were a machine whose structure produced thought, sensation, and perception, we could conceive of it as increased in size with the same proportions until one was able to enter into its interior, as he would into a mill. Now, on going into it he would find only pieces working upon one another, but never would he find anything to explain Perception.[4]

In the above passage, Leibniz uses the word "Perception" (with uppercase "P") to cover all of the various kinds of mental phenomena, or modes of awareness. Moreover, what he says here has direct application to what materialists assert concerning the brain. (It should be kept in mind that the expressions "brain" and "brain-process" are being used here in a *purely materialistic* sense; an idealist would attach a different meaning to these terms insofar as he believed them to refer to something real.)

In trying to elucidate Leibniz's example, let us alter it somewhat. Let us suppose that the machine which is allegedly capable of producing various kinds of consciousness is the brain. Now, imagine that we, as observers, are reduced in size to the point at which we are so small that we can move around among the ultimate elementary particles of which the brain consists. Let us call these ultimate elementary particles "quarks" and "electrons." As we moved among these quarks and electrons, they would appear to us to be separated by wide distances; we would encounter mainly empty space, and comparatively little solid substance. We would observe, moreover, that this multitude of quarks and electrons exhibits constant movement within a certain region of space; and, more importantly, we would note that a brain-process is nothing but a specific pattern of movement (or shift in the movement) of these quarks and electrons. Furthermore, we would see that no conceivable thought, feeling, or other mental phenomenon, could ever have the remotest resemblance to any of these brain-processes.

Let us review the main the main points that were made regarding the materialistic interpretation of premise (2). First, we noted that, according to materialism, mental phenomena depend on brain-processes in the specific sense that they JUST ARE brain-processes. Now, the view that mental phenomena JUST ARE brain processes is sometimes referred to simply as the "identity theory".   Moreover, we saw that the socalled "property objection" purports to be a conclusive refutation of the identity theory. The property objection may be stated concisely as follows: Mental phenomena JUST ARE brain-processes if and only if mental phenomena and brain-processes have all properties in common; but mental phenomena and brain-processes DO NOT have all properties in common; therefore, it is NOT the case that mental phenomena JUST ARE brain-processes.

Thus, the property objection is based on the recognition that, for any given x and y, x is identical with y if and only if x has all the properties which y has, and conversely, y has all the properties which x has. Consequently, according to the property objection, when we consider the properties of some mental phenomenon, and discover them to be totally different from the properties of brain-processes, we are justified in concluding that this mental phenomenon is not identical with any brain-process. But, is not the *feeling* of joy totally different in its properties from every conceivable brain-process? Does not the *thought* of a red rose have properties entirely different from those of brain-processes? Can we look into the brain and find anything even remotely resembling a sensation of color, sound, or pain? Insofar as the answer to these questions is "no," the conclusion seems unavoidable that these mental phenomena are not brain-processes. More generally, the property objection states that no mental phenomenon is identical with a brain-process, where the latter is understood in a purely materialistic way (i.e., as being simply the movement of material particles). By reason of the property objection, then, we are compelled to say that -- on its materialistic interpretation -- premise (2) of the brain-dependency argument is false, and consequently, the argument as a whole may be rejected.

In conclusion, whether we take the epiphenomenalist, the purely materialist, or even the emergent-materialist interpretation of "depends on," the brain-dependency argument does not succeed in disproving life after death. Therefore, while conceding the superficial appeal of this argument, the religious person may yet reasonably continue to believe in life after death.

*Notes*

[1]Russell, Bertrand, *Why I Am Not a Christian* (New York: Simon & Schuster, 1957), pp. 50 & 54.

[2]Baha'u'llah, *Gleanings from the Writings of Baha'u'llah* (Wilmette: Baha'i Publishing Trust, 1976), p. 153.

[3]Ibid., pp. 153-154. (Emphasis added.)

[4]Bcck, L. W. (ed), *18th Century Philosophy* (New York: The Free Press, 1966), p. 196.

CHAPTER NINE:

REFUTATION OF
DIRECT REALISM

CHAPTER 9: Refutation of Direct Realism

The central contention of this final chapter is the following: One of the most powerful of the factors which contribute to irreligion is a certain widespread (though fundamentally mistaken) view concerning sense-perception. More specifically, the main thesis to be developed is that certain erroneous beliefs about the process of SEEING can strongly incline us toward IRRELIGION. First, we shall try to arrive at a more definite concept of irreligion; and, subsequently, we shall turn to the problem of sense-perception.

So then, what is irreligion? That is, when a person is described as "irreligious", what essentially is the significance of that description? Before suggesting an answer to this question, I shall first address the corresponding question about the description "religious". Then, by negating the answer proposed for the latter question, an answer for the former question will have been arrived at. So, what basically do we mean when we describe a person as religious?

We may develop an answer to this question, starting from a consideration of the etymology of the word. The etymology of the word "religious" takes us back to the Latin words "re" and "ligare". The most obvious meaning of "re" is *again*, while "ligare" means *to tie together*. Thus, etymologically considered, the word "religious" conveys the idea of *tying together again*. According to one common account, this etymological meaning of the word implies that to be *religious* is to be engaged in doing, or to be disposed to do, that which will TIE one TOGETHER AGAIN with God; that is, on this view, a religious person is one who seeks to establish ANEW a LINK or CONNECTION with God. This interpretation of the etymology of "religious" is closely associated with the belief that humanity has "fallen" from some original state of union with God, to which it needs to return (hence, the reference, in this connection, to such things as the expulsion of Adam and Eve from the garden of Eden).

This particular interpretation of the etymology of "religious" doubtless does give an insight into one aspect of what it is to be religious. Nevertheless, the conceptual content of the Latin words "re" and "ligare" can also be unfolded along different lines, so as to give insight into other facets of this complex description. Accordingly, I wish to offer an alternative account of the etymology of "religious"; moreover, the answer to be proposed for the question we raised previously will be based on this alternative account.

Firstly then, instead of taking "re" as meaning *again*, let us understand it as implying the REPETITION of an action in such a way that it EXTENDS TO ALL. Now, continuing to translate "ligare" as "to tie", we can say the following: The etymology of the word "religious" suggests the idea of the TYING TOGETHER of ALL things, or, alternatively expressed, the idea that ALL things are TIED TOGETHER. In keeping with this account, we may say that being *religious* essentially involves believing, or recognizing, that ALL things are TIED TOGETHER. But, what does it mean to say that all things are tied together?

Let us understand this as a reference to bonds of *affection*. To speak of all things as being tied together is a way of stating in figurative language that ALL THINGS LOVE EACH OTHER. Now, if we take the statement "All things love each other" as equivalent to "Each thing MANIFESTLY takes delight in the reality and well-being of every other thing," then the statement "All things love each other" is obviously false. Therefore, when it is said that all things love each other, let this be understood to mean the following: EACH thing, by virtue of its ESSENTIAL NATURE, possesses ROOT-DISPOSITIONS which, although sometimes *hidden*, nonetheless, when brought to *manifestation*, cause that thing to TAKE DELIGHT in the reality and well-being of EVERY other thing. In what follows, I will, for the sake of brevity, speak simply of "love"; but, let it be kept in mind that when this single word is used, all of the above is what is intended.

The next thing to note is that such mutual love as we have envisioned has a twofold significance. That is, to say that all things love each other implies that each thing both LOVES and IS LOVED. I shall make a certain observation concerning these two facets of the mutual love of things, in turn.

Let us focus on the idea that each thing LOVES. If we grant that the ability to love is a spiritual quality, then from this idea it would logically follow that each thing is spiritual in nature. In other words, this idea is logically bound up with the notion that the entire universe is nothing but a vast multitude of spiritual beings.

According to the second aspect of the mutual love of things, each thing is LOVED. Now, for anything, x, x is loved *with justification* if and only if x is good. That is, one is not justified in loving that which is not good; rather, whatever is loved with justification is necessarily good. Therefore, from the idea that each thing is loved, insofar as this idea is conjoined with that of justification, it follows that each thing is good. In other words, this idea is inextricably bound up with the notion that each of the multitude of entities that constitute the universe is good.

Let us recapitulate. From an etymological point of view, the word "religious" conveys the idea of the tying together of all things. Moreover, to say that all things are tied together amounts to the claim that all things are UNITED by bonds of affection, that is, that all things love each other. But, if all things love each other, it follows that each things both loves and is loved. Finally, if each thing both loves and is loved, then -- given the truth of certain auxiliary assumptions -- it may be inferred that all things are SPIRITUAL and GOOD.

In keeping with the etymology-based account which we are developing, we said earlier that being *religious* essentially involves believing, or recognizing, that all things are tied together. In light of the foregoing observations, it may now be said, more explicitly, that being *religious* essentially involves the belief or recognition that all things are spiritual and good.

What is contended here is that belief in the spirituality and goodness of all things is a key ingredient in what constitutes a religious person. However, this contention does not necessarily imply that every religious person has a clear, or fully unfolded, belief in spirituality and goodness. For, it is conceivable, on this view, that the thinking of a religious person might be on a level such that this person is not as yet able to articulate the belief in spirituality and goodness in a definite way. For example, belief in the spirituality of things might take the form of a certain vague belief in the UNSEEN, an as yet unrefined sense that something invisible and intangible does indeed exist. On the other hand, belief in the goodness of things might take the form of a kind of general acceptance of the idea of Providence, the idea that all that exists, or happens, fulfills some legitimate purpose. But, irrespective of whether the belief in spirituality and goodness takes the form of a clear, rational apprehension, or simply an as yet uncultivated sense concerning the nature of things, the contention here is that being religious essentially involves such belief. Any religious person who declares, "I do not believe that all things are spiritual and good," has simply not looked deeply enough into the logical implications of what he or she does in fact believe.

These pronouncements concerning essential religiosity are wholly in agreement with the actual teachings of the various religious traditions. Consider, for instance, the following statements of Abdu'l-Baha:

> The love which exists between the hearts of believers is prompted by the ideal of the unity of spirits. This love is attained through the knowledge of God, so that men see the Divine Love reflected in the heart. Each sees in the other the Beauty of God reflected in the soul, and finding this point of similarity, they are attracted to one another in love.[1]

Consider the first sentence of the above quotation, namely "The love which exists between the hearts of believers is prompted by the *ideal* of the *unity of spirits*." Specifically, let us focus on the two parts of this passage which I have emphasized. May we take the word "ideal" as meaning *conception of perfection*, that is, consciousness of the infinite goodness of all things? What about "unity of spirits"? May we take this to mean the fact of *all spirits' being tied together*, of all spirits' being conjoined through bonds of familiarity and affection? If so, then to say that the love existing between believers is prompted by the ideal of the unity of spirits amounts to saying that this love arises, or comes to manifestation, through the consciousness that all things are infinitely good, and that this consciousness of all things as infinitely good consists in the recognition that all spirits are tied together in the sense clarified previously.  Such teachings concerning unity are--if not explicitly espoused--at least tacitly assumed in all of the major religions.  Moreover, the characteristically religious exhortation to universal benevolence (e.g., to *ahimsa* in Hinduism, to *karuna* in Buddhism, to *agape* in Christianity, or to *rahmah* and *mawaddah* in Islam) is a clear indication of this.

But let us return to our main question. In moving toward an answer to this question, two further ramifications of our etymology-based conception of religiosity may be followed out. The idea that all things are spiritual and good is logically connected with the concept of God (as the *source* of the spirituality and goodness of things), and with that of immortality (as an *outcome*, or consequence, of the spirituality and goodness of things).  For, if all things are spiritual and good, it follows that there is such a thing as *the* Spirit itself, and *the* Good itself. Moreover, if we unpack the implications of the predicates "spiritual" and "good", we shall discover that anything which is both spiritual and good is inescapably immortal. Accordingly, let us bring these points together as follows:  Being *religious* essentially involves -- among other things -- believing or recognizing that (1) All things are spiritual and good, (2) God exists, and (3) There is life after death.

Now, there is a common thread that runs through the three propositions enumerated above, namely the idea that Spirit exists. And this is the aspect of essential religiosity to which we will give special attention in the remainder of the chapter. The important point to keep in mind is that belief in the existence of Spirit is a big part of what it is to be a religious person. On the other hand, the denial of Spirit is at the heart of what it is to be irreligious. In other words, just as a characteristic belief which underlies being religious is the belief that Spirit does exist, so, similarly, the belief that Spirit does not exist (or at least the absence of the belief that Spirit does exist) lies at the foundation of irreligion.

## Theories of Sense-Perception

The next question which we need to address is this: What are the main factors which lead to irreligion? More specifically, what are some of the factors which most powerfully incline us toward the denial of Spirit? As stated at the outset, I shall contend in this chapter that certain erroneous beliefs about sense-perception, in particular the process of SEEING, are among the chief factors contributing to irreligion. More precisely, I shall maintain that such mistaken views about the process of seeing strongly incline us toward the belief that Spirit does not exist. We may begin by attempting to get clear about two general theories of the nature of sense--perception; these constitute mutually opposing views concerning sense-perception. Next, we shall note that one of the two theories leads in the direction of the denial of Spirit, while the other is conducive to the belief that Spirit does exist. Then, we shall seek through argumentation to determine the relative merits of the two theories of perception. In speaking of these theories, let us use the names "direct realism" and "the causal theory."

To begin with, we need to be altogether clear concerning the specific question to which the two theories offer opposing answers. To simplify our discussion, I will speak of one type of sense-perception only, namely vision. In formulating the question we are concerned with, we may employ the expression "visual field". By "visual field" is meant *the totality of what is seen by a seer at any given point in time.* In other words, the whole of what falls within a seer's sphere of sight at any given moment constitutes that seer's visual field. But, we need to make a distinction here. For, in the broad sense of the expression "visual field", the seer is confronted with a visual field both during the waking state and during the state of dreaming. Our question concerns the status of the visual field in relation to the seer, and more specifically, the status of that visual field which confronts the seer during the state of waking-consciousness. As we reflect on this, let each of us think in terms of the grammatical "first person singular," i.e., I. We may put the question as follows: What exactly is the status of my visual field in relation to me, the *unseen* seer, when I happen to be awake? Does my visual field then consist of a set of INDEPENDENT objects entirely distinct from my consciousness, or is my visual field simply MY OWN CONSCIOUSNESS, and hence, something which is inseparably connected to me, the seer?

The direct realist theory of perception affirms the former possibility. That is, according to direct realism, the visual field of each seer consists of a set of independent objects entirely distinct from his/her consciousness. On this view, each of the multitude of *color-expanses* which confront the seer during waking consciousness is actually a part of the *surface of a material thing*, and as such has an existence SEPARATE-AND-DISTINCT from the seer. This, of course, is just the ordinary way of thinking about visual sense-perception; it is the common view of the process of seeing. In fact, it seems clear that, pre-philosophically, it would never even occur to the vast majority of persons that the actual truth about seeing might possibly be something other than what direct realism asserts. For, pre-philosophically, it seems *just obvious* that the process of seeing amounts to a direct apprehension of independently-existing objects. Therefore, to become altogether clear about the meaning of "direct realism," it will suffice if we simply take note of what we have all, more or less automatically, come to believe about the process of seeing. In other words, once we have begun to engage in philosophic reflection, the majority of us will discover that we ALREADY have been holding to certain beliefs about what sort of process seeing is, and it is to these beliefs that the designation "direct realism" applies.

The causal theory, on the other hand, portrays the process of seeing as something entirely different from what we commonly suppose it to be. (The expression "causal theory" can be used differently from how I use it here; however, in the present discussion, it should be understood in the sense I shall STIPULATE below.) According to the causal theory, the visual field of each seer is simply that seer's OWN CONSCIOUSNESS, and, thus, something inseparably connected to the seer. On this view, during normal waking consciousness, each seer is directly confronted only with mind-pictures, mind-pictures fundamentally similar to those which are experienced during a dream. However, on the causal theory, the mental pictures which are experienced during the state of wakeful seeing differ in one very important respect from the mental pictures which arise during a dream. During the state of waking-consciousness, all of the sequentially-appearing mind-pictures which constitute the successive states of the seer's visual field are IMPRESSIONS received from outside of the seer. According to the causal theory of sense-perception, the mind-pictures of wakeful seeing do not arise in the seer in an arbitrary fashion. Rather, these mind-pictures are visual impressions which arise within the seer's consciousness in accordance with definite laws; more specifically, they are CAUSALLY INDUCED upon the seer's consciousness in conformity with what is required by the actual nature of EXTERNAL THINGS and OCCURRENCES.

Let me try to clarify the latter point by means of a comparison.

Consider the pictures which appear on the screen of a television. The pictures on a television screen arise in conformity with the nature of certain remote things and occurrences. That is, the pictures that appear on the television screen REPRESENT certain entities and events at a great distance away from the television set, namely the persons and things in the TV studio or place from which the transmission originates. And it is precisely these distant things and occurrences which ultimately GIVE RISE to the pictures which appear on the screen. Now, the point of this analogy is this: Just as the television has its screen, so the "I" (the ego or soul) has its visuality, and in recognition of this visuality, we refer to the "I" as seer. The visuality of the "I" is simply the visual portion of that potency which the "I" possesses as a conscious entity; it is the capacity of the "I" for color-perception. Briefly, the visuality of the "I" is analogous to the screen of the television. Accordingly, just as certain pictures appear on the television screen which are CAUSED by, and which REPRESENT, *remote* things and occurrences, so, similarly, the mind-pictures which arise through the visuality of the "I" are assumed to be CAUSED by and, in some sense, to REPRESENT things and occurrences which are altogether *beyond* the visual field of the seer. In short, according to the causal theory, the process of seeing is one in which the seer in never directly confronted with external things, but rather with mind-pictures only, but, nonetheless, these mind-pictures are caused by external things, and hence, in some way represent such external things.

Now, even dating back to the earliest periods of history, philosophers have recognized the causal theory of sense-perception as a possible alternative to the direct realist view. Nevertheless, because of its counter-intuitive character, and in particular because its conception of SEEING so drastically deviates from what seeing seems to be, the causal theory has never been widely accepted as true. The reason for this is that the opposing view, direct realism, has a powerful *appearance* of correctness, an appearance which it is not at all easy to shake off. For, direct realism states that seeing IS exactly what it SEEMS to be, i.e., that it is a *direct* confrontation of the seer with independent entities, i.e., external objects. Indeed, it is an extremely difficult thing--even for highly trained philosophers-- to come to the point of realizing that seeing may in fact not be the kind of process that it SEEMS to be when superficially considered.

I said at the outset of this chapter that a certain mistaken view about seeing is a significant factor making for irreligion. It should now be clear that I was alluding to the direct realist account of seeing. That is, the direct realist understanding of the process of seeing tends to lead in the direction of the denial of Spirit. More explicitly put, insofar as one supposes that seeing gives DIRECT access to independent objects (i.e., to objects that actually exist outside of the mind of the seer), the idea that Spirit exists is correspondingly difficult to accept. For, if to see is veritably to be *directly* confronted with real, external things, then seeing by itself should be sufficient to reveal to us the true nature of the external world, that is, the external world should possess the very characteristics which are revealed in the act of seeing. But, if the external world does possess the very characteristics which are revealed in seeing, then it would seem that the whole external world must be material in character. And if the whole external world (i.e., the totality of what exists outside of the consciousness of the seer) is material in character, then it would appear that there is no room in the universe for anything that is *spiritual* in character. Thus, it is clear that direct realism tends to lead toward the conclusion that Spirit does not exist, which is to say, it is a factor making for irreligion. Later I will try to show that the causal theory has the opposite tendency, i.e., that it is conducive to the belief that Spirit does exist. But let us first look at some of the reasons which have been advanced against direct realism.

## The Argument from Illusion

The particular argument that we shall consider is the one which is most significant historically; it is the so-called "argument from illusion." From as far back as the ancient Greeks down to the present day, the argument from illusion has been among the chief arguments which philosophers have relied on to establish that seeing does not in reality give that direct access to things which pre-philosophically it seems to. In examining the relevant literature, one discovers that the actual formulations of this argument vary substantially from one philosopher to another; however, in most instances attention is focused on certain cases of relativity in the size or shape of visible objects. The specific formulation which I shall present below is based on a case of relativity in the immediately apprehended size of visible objects.

Imagine the following situation. You are sitting alone in a classroom at some university. For, you have decided to attend a certain public lecture, and have arrived somewhat early at the place where the lecture is to be given. Since no one else is there, you have an unobstructed view of everything in the classroom. While you are waiting for the speaker and the rest of the audience to arrive, you happen to look toward the front of the classroom; there, up against the wall directly across from where you are seated, you notice a chair. At that point, you hold up your hand in front of you and look at it while simultaneously looking at the chair. Then, to get a better view of the two together, you close one of your eyes. You now compare the size of the chair with the size of your hand. You see that the "chair" is smaller than your "hand." Next, you get up from your seat, walk over to the chair, and place your hand on it. And when you again compare the size of the "chair" with the size of your "hand," you see that the "chair" is now larger than your "hand." But then you return to your seat and compare the two again; now you notice that the "chair" has gone back to being smaller than your "hand".

Now, if you were actually to do the things set forth in the above imaginary situation, you would discover that the results would be precisely what I have indicated. That is, the "chair" would at first be seen as smaller than your hand, then as larger than your hand, and finally as once again smaller that your hand. And the question to ask is: How is this possible? For, in spite of the fact that seeing seems to show us that the chair has CHANGED, we suppose, nonetheless, that no real change has occurred in the size of the chair; that is, we assume that the mere fact of being seen from different distances does not actually cause the chair to change its size. An especially good example of this same phenomenon is the case of a "huge" airplane which--from a distance--is seen as a tiny speck moving across the sky. But, more generally, *everything* that we see is seen as comparatively large when we are near to it, and as comparatively small when we are farther away from it. Nevertheless, we do not commonly suppose that changing our distance in relation to things actually causes things to change their size. Moreover, all formulations of what is called the argument from illusion are based on such cases of perceptual relativity as that which I have described.

Using the case of a chair-as-seen-from-a-distance, we may state the argument from illusion as follows:

PART I
(1) Premise: What I see when I look at a chair from a distance is *smaller* than my hand.
(2) Premise: The real chair, that is, that external thing itself, is *larger* than my hand.
CONCLUSION: Therefore, what I see when I look at a chair from a

distance is not the real chair, that is, is not the external thing itself.

PART II

(1) Premise:  If direct realism is true, then what I see when I look at a chair from a distance is the real chair, that is, the external thing itself.

(2) Premise:  As established in PART I above, what I see when I look at a chair from a distance is NOT the real chair, that is, is NOT the external thing itself.

CONCLUSION:  Therefore, direct realism is NOT true.

Let us consider another case of perceptual relativity. Suppose that you are standing on a certain street, and that you look down the street, far into the distance, and see the rear portion of a metrobus parked at a curb. You raise your hand with your thumb positioned upward, and then, looking at your thumb together with the metrobus, you compare them as to size. As in the former case, you close one of your eyes in order to be able to see the two alongside each other more clearly. You now notice that the metrobus is appreciably smaller than your thumb. Assume, moreover, that at the very moment when you are taking note of this, the bus driver is standing behind his bus comparing its size with the size of his thumb in precisely the same manner in which you are doing this. However, what the bus driver sees is substantially larger than his thumb. Using this particular example, we can formulate the argument from illusion as follows:

PART I

(1) Premise:  What I see when I look at the bus is *smaller* than a human thumb.

(2) Premise:  What the bus driver sees when he looks at the bus is *larger* than a human thumb.

CONCLUSION:  Therefore, what I see when I look at the bus and what the bus driver sees when he looks at the bus are NOT one and the same thing.

PART II

(1) Premise.  If direct realism is true, then what I see when I look at the bus and what the bus driver sees when he looks at the bus are one and the same thing.

(2) Premise:  But, as established in PART I above, what I see when I look at the bus and what the bus driver sees when he looks at the bus are NOT one and the same thing.

CONCLUSION:   Therefore, direct realism is NOT true.

Now, there is a certain objection which some philosophers have regarded as decisive against the argument from illusion. We shall digress briefly in order to examine this objection; for, the argument from illusion is the chief argument on which I am relying in my attempt at refuting direct realism. One of the philosophers who raised this objection is G. E. Moore. Using the term "sense-datum" to refer to what we directly confront in the process of seeing (and in other sensory processes), Moore states this criticism of the argument from illusion as follows:

> What now seems to me to be possible is that the sense-datum which corresponds to a tree, which I am seeing, when I am a mile off, may not really be perceived to *be* smaller than the one, which corresponds to the same tree, when I see it from a distance of only a hundred yards, but that it is only perceived to *seem* smaller; that the sense-datum which corresponds to a penny, which I am seeing obliquely, is not really perceived to *be* different in shape from that which corresponded to the penny, when I was straight in front of it, but is only perceived to *seem* different--that all that is perceived is that the one seems elliptical and the other circular ... [2]

Another recent philosopher who has attacked the argument from illusion is G. J. Warnock. He raises essentially the same objection that Moore raises in the above quotation. The immediate target of Warnock's assault is the philosopher George Berkeley. He states his criticism as follows:

> But secondly, Berkeley makes a most curious assumption. He asserts in the course of his argument that if some property were 'really inherent' in an object, the object would necessarily *appear* to have that property in all circumstances. This extraordinary assumption, which entirely disregards the importance of the *conditions in which* objects are observed and of the question by *whom* they are observed, needs only to be stated clearly to be seen to be absurd ... It is only fair to say, however, that more than one modern philosopher has either stated this as his own opinion, or represented it as the opinion of ordinary men. It might be suggested that, unless this fantastic assumption is made, the 'argument from illusion' cannot get started; for unless we begin by supposing that things *cannot* appear to be otherwise than they are, why should we be at all put out by the

obvious fact that they can and do.[3]

In short, a significant number of contemporary philosophers have voiced what is basically the same objection. Thus, we also find J. L. Austin[4] and I. C. Tipton[5] rejecting the argument from illusion for reasons very similar to those delineated in the preceding quotations. Indeed, from the standpoint of commonsense assumptions about sense-perception, this particular criticism is the most obvious one to raise. In the ensuing discussion, I shall refer to it simply as "the criticism."

To facilitate our discussion of the criticism, let us focus on one specific case of perceptual relativity, keeping in mind that whatever is asserted in connection with this particular case has applicability to all other cases of such perceptual relativity. We may employ the example of the "elliptical penny" alluded to in the Moore quotation. Using this example, the argument from illusion may be stated as follows:

(1) Premise: What I see when I look at a penny from an angle is *elliptical* in shape.
(2) Premise: The real penny, that is, the external thing itself is *circular* in shape.
CONCLUSION: Therefore, what I see when I look at a penny from an angle is NOT the real penny, that is, is NOT the external thing itself.

Let us return to the criticism. In the various formulations of the criticism by different writers, the expressions "seems," "appears," and "looks" are used interchangeably. In the following remarks, I shall stick with "looks." Now, the central thesis of the criticism--as it is applicable to the case of the "elliptical penny"--is this: Even though what I see when I look at a penny from an angle LOOKS elliptical, it does not follow from this that it actually IS elliptical. Thus, according to the criticism, proponents of the argument from illusion are led astray through erroneously assuming that simply because the penny *looks* elliptical from a certain angle, it therefore must *be* elliptical. In other words, the core of the criticism consists in the claim that premise (1) of the argument from illusion, as stated above, is false. For the sake of concision, let us use the letter x to symbolize the somewhat cumbersome expression "what I see when I look at a penny from an angle". We may now state the criticism as follows:

(1) Premise:  If the sentence "x looks elliptical" does not imply the sentence "x is elliptical", then premise (1) of the argument from illusion is false.

(2) Premise:  The sentence "x looks elliptical" in fact does not imply the sentence x is elliptical".

CONCLUSION:     Therefore, premise (1) of the argument from illusion is false.

Now, if we think carefully concerning premise (2) of the criticism, we will discover that this claim constitutes its main weakness. More specifically, in stating that "looks" does not imply "is," opponents of the argument from illusion show that they have misunderstood the argument's references to "*What I see* when I look at a penny from an angle." For, when the argument from illusion refers to *what I see* when I look at a penny from an angle, this is intended in a purely phenomenological sense. Phenomenology involves describing the actual contents of IMMEDIATE CONSCIOUSNESS. Thus, in a phenomenological sense, the expression "*what I see* when I look at a penny from an angle" must be taken to mean that which I am IMMEDIATELY CONSCIOUS of when I look at the penny. Moreover, any assumption concerning the significance, or meaning, of that of which I am immediately conscious would amount to an INTERPRETATION of immediate experience, and as such would *go beyond* a purely phenomenological account.

If I simply describe, in a purely phenomenological way, what I see when I look at a penny from an angle, I am compelled to say that *what I see* not only looks elliptical, but actually IS elliptical. A phenomenologically pure description would be exactly the same as the description which would be given by a person born blind who suddenly gained the ability to see. That is, when I look at a penny from an angle, what I see, in a purely phenomenological sense, consists of that which I am IMMEDIATELY CONSCIOUS of, not that which I have learned automatically to INFER. And what I am immediately conscious of when I look at a penny from an angle includes only that which would be mentioned in the description of a person born blind who suddenly became sighted, and whose first visual experience was that of looking at a penny from an angle. Such a newly sighted person, upon looking at a penny from an angle, would surely be aware only of an elliptical shape, so that consciousness of circularity would not arise at al

Similarly, what I see in a purely *phenomenological* sense, that is, what I am IMMEDIATELY CONSCIOUS of when looking at the penny, not only looks elliptical, but actually IS elliptical. To express this in a more general way, if we let p stand for any predicate, then, from a purely phenomenological standpoint, whatever *looks* p actually *is* p. Accordingly, in this sense, a chair *as seen* from a distance not only looks smaller than my hand, but actually IS smaller than my hand; that is, it i smaller, as seen by me, or *as represented to my visual consciousness*. In the same way, a metro-bus as seen from a distance not only looks smaller than my thumb, but actually IS smaller than my thumb. From these considerations, it follows that premise (2) of the criticism is true only in a sense which is not relevant to the argument from illusion. Consequently, the criticism does not succeed as a refutation of the argument from illusion.

But, there is another difficulty with the argument from illusion, namely this: The argument in the form in which it is ordinarily stated, is self-canceling. For, the conclusion of the argument implies that the real penny, that is, the *external* penny itself, cannot be directly seen; moreover, in order to arrive at this conclusion, we needed the premise "The real penny is circular". But, in order to be able to verify that the real penny is circular, we have to be able to see the real penny itself. Hence, it is clear that the conclusion of the argument implies that there is no possibility of verifying the very premise through which that conclusion was arrived at. And in this sense the argument from illusion can be said to be self-canceling; for, one part of the argument (the conclusion), so to speak, cancels out another part of it (the second premise).

In order to get around this particular difficulty it is necessary to alter the manner in which the argument from illusion is stated. Consider the following alternative formulation:

PART I
(1) Premise: What I see when I look at a penny from an angle is elliptical in shape.
(2) Premise: What I see when I look at a penny from straight over head is circular.
CONCLUSION: Therefore, what I see when I look at a penny from an angle and what I see when I look at a penny from straight over head are NOT *one and the same* thing.
PART II

(1) Premise: If direct realism is true, then what I see when I look at a penny from an angle is *one and the same* thing as what I see when I look at a penny from straight over head.

(2) Premise: But, as established in PART I above, what I see when I look at a penny from an angle is NOT *one and the same* thing as what I see when I look at a penny from straight over head.

CONCLUSION: Therefore, direct realism is NOT true.

If we transform the argument from illusion in the above manner, then our conclusion is no longer such that its truth would preclude the possibility of our having any means by which to verify a crucial premise through which that conclusion was reached in the first place. Through this transformation, the elliptical-penny formulation of the argument from illusion becomes in a certain respect comparable to the metrobus formulation we looked at earlier, and therefore, ceases to be self-canceling. Consequently, the argument from illusion is able to withstand this second objection also.

Let us now look at the argument from illusion in a slightly different way. So far, we have been examining it as a means by which to prove that direct realism is not true. When we approach the matter in this way, there is no direct reference to the *mind-dependent* status of visible objects. I shall now attempt to bring out in a more explicit manner certain connections which exist between the phenomenon of illusions and the proposition that what the seer confronts in the process of seeing is inseparably connected to the seer, i.e., is mind-dependent. In doing this, I shall develop the argument from illusion along lines that differ considerably from those of the usual account.

Using the penny-example, my main point may be stated as follows: The established non-identity of what I see from an angle with what I see from straight over head can BEST BE EXPLAINED by the assumption that all visible objects are mind-dependent. Moreover, this mind-dependency assumption is the BEST explanation primarily by reason of the fact that through it we are able to avoid having to address the question: "Where" is the elliptical expanse when the circular expanse confronts the seer, and conversely, "where" is the circular expanse when the elliptical expanse confronts the seer?

Let me try to state more clearly what I am getting at. The problem is this: What is the significance of saying that the mind-dependency assumption provides the *best* account of the non-identity of the elliptical and circular expanses? Or, in other words, in what does the betterness of the mind-dependency account consist? First of all, suppose it is true that what I see from an angle is not one and the same thing as what I see from directly over head. Suppose, moreover, that we may take one or the other of two opposing views concerning the "status" of such immediately-visible objects. We may refer to the one view as the "mind-dependency assumption," and the other as the "duality assumption." The mind-dependency assumption asserts that immediately-visible objects are mind-dependent in the sense of being *inseparably connected* to the consciousness of the seer; this is the central claim of the causal theory. On the other hand, the duality assumption maintains that immediately-visible objects are mind-independent in the sense of being separate-and distinct from the consciousness of the seer, this is the central claim of direct realism.

Now, given that the elliptical expanse apprehended from an angle cannot be one and the same thing as the circular expanse which is apprehended from straight over head (because ellipticality and circularity are mutually incompatible properties), should we accept the mind-dependency assumption, or the duality assumption? If the duality assumption is correct, then each of the (non-identical) visible objects is mind-independent, that is, both the elliptical expanse and the circular expanse are separate-and-distinct from the consciousness of the seer. Moreover, if each of these expanses is independent of the seer, then each expanse exists not only while it is being seen, but also AFTER IT HAS CEASED TO BE SEEN. Therefore, if we adopt the duality assumption, then we are forced to say that, when the seer successively views a penny from different angles, certain *independent* entities are successively presented to that seer's consciousness, and that each of these independent entities CONTINUES TO EXIST even after it is no longer present to the seer's consciousness, that is, no longer seen by the seer. Now, if we are forced to say this, then we incur the following difficulty: What becomes of the circular expanse when the seer is confronted with the elliptical expanse, and conversely, what has become of the elliptical expanse when the seer is confronted with the circular expanse? In other words, if it is true that the circular expanse which I previously apprehended is still in existence at the time when I am confronted with the elliptical expanse, then "where" is the circular expanse at that time? On the other hand, if the elliptical still exists when I am confronted with the circular, then "where" is the elliptical at that time? If viewing a penny successively from different angles involves the successive presentation to consciousness of certain self-existent, or independent, entities, then what is the status of these entities BEFORE and AFTER they are presented to consciousness? (Remember: We are taking for granted that the elliptical expanse and the circular expanse are NOT identical, but rather TWO DIFFERENT things.) I submit that there is no way this difficulty incurred by the duality assumption can be resolved. Consequently, given that the elliptical expanse apprehended from an angle and the circular expanse apprehended from straight over head are not the same thing, the duality assumption must be rejected.

This difficulty can be avoided if we adopt the mind-dependency assumption. Once again, let us take it as established that what is seen from an angle cannot be one and the same thing as what is seen from straight over head (for what is elliptical cannot be identical with what is circular). Now, how do we explain this fact? How do we account for the fact that what we had thought to be one and the same thing has turned out in reality to be TWO DIFFERENT things? If we adopt the mind-dependency assumption, we have the following explanation: As the seer views the penny from different angles there is a successive *production* in the seer's consciousness of certain *mind-pictures*, mind-pictures which cease to exist upon ceasing to be apprehended. On this view, it is not necessary to assume the successive *presentation* to consciousness of *independent entities*, entities existing both before and after they have ceased to be apprehended; and, consequently, we do not incur the difficulty discussed above. In other words, if viewing the penny from different angles involves a successive *production* in the seer's consciousness of certain TEMPORARILY-existing mind-pictures, then the question "Where are these mind-pictures when they are not being apprehended?" does not arise. For, in that case, the elliptical "production" simply does not exist when the circular is seen, and conversely, the circular "production" does not exist when the elliptical is seen. The upshot of these considerations is this: The "betterness" of the mind-dependency assumption as an explanation consists in the fact that if we adopt it, then we can offer an account of the antecedently established non-identity, and at the same time avoid the difficulty incurred by the duality assumption.

## A Source of Religiosity

I intimated earlier that just as direct realism tends to be conducive to the denial of Spirit, and thus to irreligion, so, by contrast, the causal theory tends to lead toward the belief in Spirit, and hence, is a factor which can increase the likelihood of religiosity. For, if the causal theory is correct, and in particular if its mind-dependency assumption is true, then this fact provides rational support for the proposition "Spirit does exist." Consequently, the recognition of this fact of mind-dependency would facilitate our developing the distinctive modes of thinking (i.e., *spiritual* modes of thinking) that differentiate religious persons from those who are irreligious.

Now, on one level, we have already dealt with the problem of proving the existence of Spirit. Specifically, we noted in Chapter 5 that one can arrive at the conviction that Spirit exists through SELF-CONTEMPLATION. That is, by means of appropriate introspection, or "looking inward," I can gradually come to the point of grasping myself as innermost "I", and through the continuation of such self-observation I can eventually arrive at the point of understanding that this "I," my essential self, is purely spiritual in nature. Moreover, since my own existence is certain, I can acquire in this way the conviction that SPIRIT DOES EXIST.

But, we can also approach this question from a different direction, namely through a consideration of the possible ramifications of the causal theory of sense-perception. In this connection, the fundamental point to keep in mind is this: According to the causal theory, the entire visual field of each seer is nothing but that seer's own consciousness, and consequently, seeing does not give the seer DIRECT access to the external world. This implies that the seer's visual field is comparable to a kind of curtain, or barrier, that keeps him/her from immediately apprehending the TRUE CHARACTER of the external world. In other words, if the mind-dependency assumption is correct, then the real world is hidden BEHIND this "curtain," i.e., BEHIND the seer's visual field. (It should be remembered, in reflecting on these various points, that the seer's visual field includes the TOTALITY of what the seer sees; therefore, all the things encountered at the center of the visual field, which the seer describes, for example, as the "tip of my nose," "my arms," "my legs," "my entire body," etc., are just parts of the barrier or curtain.) Consequently, the seer cannot find out the TRUE NATURE of the external world merely by considering the nature of what is displayed as the visual field.

If seeing were actually the kind of process which it SEEMS to be, that is, if seeing really amounted to a *direct* confrontation with the outside world, then there would basically be no mystery about the nature of external things; on the contrary, the question, "What is the nature of the external world?" would have an OBVIOUS answer. For, if seeing is a direct process, then the external world has the very characteristics *which we see*. And what we see are characteristics such as size, shape, color, position, and so forth. But, if such characteristics as these belong to INDEPENDENT things, it follows that such independent things are MATERIAL objects; and so, we are led to the conclusion that the world is made of MATTER.

On the other hand, if the causal theory is correct, then seeing is NOT a direct apprehension of external things. And if seeing does not give direct access to the external world, i.e., if the real world is hidden BEHIND the curtain of the visual field, then this raises the possibility that real external things might have characteristics altogether different from those which, so to speak, appear on the curtain. In other words, the truth of the causal theory would open up the possibility that the real world might not be made of matter.

Thus, the question becomes: What is the nature of those things which are concealed behind the visual field, behind the "curtain?" It cannot reasonably be answered: The things *behind* this curtain are OBVIOUSLY *material* things. Perhaps the outer world, the world hidden behind this curtain, is not made of matter; it may be that this outer world is, at least in part, possessed of a spiritual nature. It is even conceivable that this outer world consists of spiritual beings ONLY. But, in any event, to interpose a barrier between the seer and the external world, as the causal theory does, makes it much easier to believe that the various kinds of realities posited by religions (e.g., God, divinities, angels, ancestors, heaven, purgatory, hell, and so on) might possibly exist. That is, if the real external universe is concealed behind the visual field of each seer, so that its true character can never be immediately accessed by seeing, then to argue as follows is simply not reasonable: Since I cannot *see* God, angels, heaven, etc., it is doubtful that such things exist. For, if I argue in this way, then-- assuming that the causal theory is correct--I am guilty of the mistake of thinking that the world actually CONSISTS OF that which confronts me as my visual field.

Perhaps the things which are SEEN are merely fleeting occurrences on the screen of visuality, while the things that are NOT SEEN are true and eternal "substances," that is, the very realities which the universe is made of. That is the main point which I wanted to stress in this chapter. Moreover, this theme is beautifully set forth by the Apostle Paul in a certain passage from his second epistle to the Corinthians. I cite it here as a fitting note on which to end these reflections: "For our light affliction, which is but for a moment, worketh for us a far more exceeding and eternal weight of glory; While we look not at the things which are SEEN, but at the things which are NOT SEEN: for the things which are SEEN are temporal; but the things which are NOT SEEN are eternal." (II Corinthians, Chapter 4, 17-18 [emphasis added])

*Notes*

[1]Abdu 'l-Baha, *Paris Talks* (Wilmette: Baha 'i Publishing Trust, 1969), pp. 180-181.

[2]Swartz, R. J. (ed.), *Perceiving, Sensing, and Knowing* (New York: Doubleday, 1965), pp. 22-23.

[3]Warnock, G. J., *Berkeley* (London: Peregrine edition, 1969), p. 148.

[4]Austin, J. L., *Sense and Sensibilia* (Oxford: Clarendon Press, 1962).

[5]Tipton, I. C., *Berkeley* (London: Methuen & Co., 1974).

# INDEX